CREATED *for* COVERING

Understanding the Concept of
Safety and Covering In Relationships
for Men and Women

Robert B. Shaw, Jr.

With a Foreword by Dr. Mark Chironna, Ph.D.

WESTBOW
PRESS®
A DIVISION OF THOMAS NELSON
& ZONDERVAN

WestBow Press books may be ordered through booksellers or by contacting:

WestBow Press
A Division of Thomas Nelson & Zondervan
1663 Liberty Drive
Bloomington, IN 47403
www.westbowpress.com
1 (866) 928-1240

ISBN: 978-1-4497-8275-7 (sc)
ISBN: 978-1-4497-8276-4 (hc)
ISBN: 978-1-4497-8274-0 (e)

Library of Congress Control Number: 2013901244

Print information available on the last page.

Unless otherwise indicated, Bible quotations are taken from the New American Standard Version of the Bible. © 1999, Zondervan Publishing House.

All names used are fictitious, and do not represent the real names of the individuals.

WestBow Press rev. date: 4/15/2016

Dedication

To my dear wife, Lorinda, and to my wonderful children, Aaron, Kenneth, April, Jeremy, and Bonnie, who have put up with me as I grow into a responsible coverer.

Thanks be to my Lord Jesus Christ, Whose grace, protection, and faithfulness continue to cover me and orchestrate the unfolding of my life.

Contents

Foreword	Bishop Mark J. Chironna, Ph.D.	ix
Introduction		xiii
Chapter 1	In the Beginning—God's Design	1
Chapter 2	Divine Delegation	10
Chapter 3	Covering for Men	16
Chapter 4	Covering for Women	33
Chapter 5	Covering versus Controlling	53
Chapter 6	When the Covering Is Lost	62
Chapter 7	How to Restore the Covering	82
Chapter 8	As It Should Be: A Summary	94
References		107

Foreword

Our ability to achieve our full potential as God has intended requires relationship and connectivity. At the most elementary level, the kingdom of God, which is in the Holy Spirit, is all about relationship. As a matter of fact, everything in the kingdom is related. Failure to understand that leads to missed opportunities, missed moments, and even missed destinies. The psalmist tells us that "God places the solitary in families," and that He is a Father to the "fatherless." So, from heaven's perspective, right relationship involves being connected to a family. No one needs to read too many news headlines or watch too many "reality" television shows to realize that families are in trouble, men and women are in crisis in regards to their masculinity and femininity, and confusion about roles and functions in our social containers is prevalent. In fact, we live in an hour when all of our social containers are in chaos, from the family to the church or synagogue, the community, and sadly even our elected officials, who are assigned to govern the affairs of life on our behalf and uphold the will of the people. We live in an hour when the masses are feeling out of sync, out of sorts, and even out of touch. We are far more vulnerable in this hour than we are visionary. There is hope, however, to reclaim, recover, and recommit to principles that actually restore balance and equilibrium to our lives. My dear friend, Dr. Robert Shaw, has decided to "take on" the sometimes perplexing and controversial concept of "covering"

in terms of its purpose in relationships in the kingdom of God. There is no question that for some, a great deal of damage was done when those in authority, who themselves had by sheer determination, performance orientation, and the will to succeed, achieved levels of leadership in the body of Christ without the character to match the positions they held. Their promotions were based on their ability to move a crowd, preach a good sermon or make a good speech, and convince others that they had what it takes to lead, only to discover, once they had arrived at the position they had sought to attain, that there was a painfully evident "gap" between their position and their "person." The result was, and always is, that instead of offering *security*, *safety*, and *protection* (i.e., "covering") for those under their care, they operated and still operate in a spirit of "control," so that "covering" has become a lid to oppress and hold people under instead of an umbrella to provide shelter from the storms of life. Covering is God's idea. Sadly, there has been so much dysfunction prevalent in the lives of the masses both churched and un-churched in recent decades that covering has lost its significance, its essence, and its essential necessity in the lives of far too many people. Individuals out of their own dysfunction, have opted for independence as opposed to interdependence in every social container, from the family all the way to the highest levels of government. If ever families, churches, communities, governments, and nations needed to recover a genuine, healthy, God-centered, wholesome awareness and experience of "covering," the time is now.

My deepest appreciation goes to Dr. Shaw for taking the time to instruct us, both theologically and psychologically from a wealth of his own personal history and experience in the people-helping business, regarding this important truth and its appropriate application to our lives. Take your time as you read this "learning manual," and once you read it, do what it says to do. Your life and the lives of those related to you will all benefit from it, because once you become the change you desire to see, others begin to experience that same transformation.

Bishop Mark J. Chironna, M.A., Ph.D.
Church on the Living Edge
Mark Chironna Ministries
Orlando, Florida

Introduction

S afety: All individuals want to know that they are safe and secure. It is one of the six core longings, (safety; significance; purpose; belonging; understanding; and love) introduced in the previous 'Created for Significance" book. People spend a lot of money on home security systems or personal weapons for their home. Neighborhood watches are popular in many communities. Schools are now seeking ways to keep their children safe while on campus, especially in light of school violence and shootings that have taken place at places like Columbine High School in Colorado, and Sandy Hook Elementary School in Connecticut. Automobile companies go to great lengths to engineer and develop safety features for their cars. Companies that manufacture strollers and baby car seats have made products that provide as much safety as possible for our children. Even in the military, training and weaponry is designed to minimize the aspect of placing our military personnel in harms' way, if possible. Factories and business firms teach safety in the work place as a part of their orientation for new employees. Sexual and physical harassment accusations are usually taken seriously and have zero tolerance, in order to assure the employee of a safe environment in which to work. Financial plans, budgets, and retirement accounts are designed to provide a safe and secure futures in good times and difficult times. Our personal belongings, our loved ones, and our relationships are important, and we desire safety and security for all.

For example, Tanya Metaksa in her book, "Safe, Not Sorry" (1997), provides many details as to how to be safe in several different times and places. Here are some basic helps:

Home Security
- Use 1.5 inch case-hardened steel deadbolts on doors
- Use timer lights, motion detector lights; keep shrubs trimmed so as to not provide a place for intruders to hide behind
- Use battery powered or third party monitoring system; even a medium size dog can be a deterrent
- Never give entire key chain to car mechanic – only car key

Travel Security
- If hotel clerk calls out your room number, ask for another room
- Carry mace
- Rental cars should have no identifying marks or stickers
- Have neighbors collect your mail, take in garbage cans, keep grass cut

Phone Security
- Do not buy over the phone from anyone you do not know or cannot verify
- Leave generic phone message; if you are a single woman, have a male friend provide the voice on your phone message
- List your name in phone book under a different name or use initials for your first and middle names, so when someone calls you asking for the name in the phone book, you know he or she is a stranger

Automotive Security
- Have your keys ready to open your car door as you approach – (electronic keys are the best)
- Do not spend several minutes listening to music while parked; if you are a woman, do not spend several minutes

putting on makeup while parked – leave from where you are as soon as possible
- Walk to your car with your head up, looking around you, not with head down as if you were trying to hide in the open
- Know how to read a map, not just a GPS

Physical Security
- Use your instincts and honor your "red flags"
- Don't be afraid to scream if necessary
- ATMs – use ATMs near lighting, indoors, in grocery stores, drive-throughs; no secluded ATMs
- Parking garages – keep one hand free at all times; use ramps, not cramped stairwells
- If you feel you are being followed while driving, do not go home – call police or drive to police or fire station
- Know the bell button on elevators; if someone brushes up against you, leave the area
- Jogging – use club or home treadmill as a preference; if you do jog outside, know your surroundings, don't jog alone, do not use iPod if by yourself; be careful what you wear – while you have the right to wear whatever, criminals do not care about your rights, they are "sight feeders"
- Purses – keep money, license, ID in a pocket, not purse if possible; if someone wants your purse, let it go – don't fight for it – the quicker you place distance between you and the thief, the better and safer for you

Safety in relationships, the subject of this book, is perhaps the most needed and less prepared for environment than any other. Relationships are the foundation of families and cultures. We can all do well to learn what to look for in someone to feel safe in their presence. We can all benefit from learning policies and values of individuals, groups, and even governments in order to determine the choices we make as to where to live, who to spend time with, and what environments to choose to be a part of. Leaders, whether they be in the workplace, in the government, in churches, in the community, or in the home, need to understand the longing we all have to be safe. Consequences are deep and wide when someone feels safe, as well as when someone has just been hurt, abused, or mistreated. Those who follow leaders want to know that their well-being is important to those they choose to follow. All of us desire safety in our relationships.

We have often heard about leadership concepts in many arenas, such as in the marketplace, politics, and even in religious institutions. Recent concepts such as "mentoring" or "coaching" are very popular and relatively effective for corporate executives and ministry leaders alike.

We also hear of various types of leaders, such as "visionaries," or "administrators" or "charismatic" leaders, to name a few. All these types of leaders possess certain characteristics that help them be very effective within their spheres of influence.

Corporations will spend millions of dollars training industry leaders. Churches have seminaries and mentoring programs that help train pastors, missionaries, and other ministry leaders and coordinators. All training has the goal of helping people become competent in their roles. A competent leader will usually elicit the feelings of security and safety among those under his or her care. However, in my experience and observations over the years as a business manager in the secular world, as a church leader and as a professional counselor, one major area is lacking in leader development. In my opinion, correct and appropriate male leadership *in the home*, has been missing. An overlooked aspect of leadership, which begins in the home, is *safety*. The home is supposed to be safe. Safety breeds love, security, and protection but also the environment to dream, be creative, and pursue the God-given destiny of all involved. As a result, our society, along with other cultures, has seen many negative effects. Stay with me: Allow me to explain.

Strong nations are made up of strong states or regions, which are supported by strong cities and communities, which are supported by strong churches, which ultimately are comprised of strong families. This is not my idea, but has been God's design from the very beginning. However, our adversary, the devil, knows that if families are weakened, a chain reaction throughout a culture takes place, resulting in weaknesses at every level.

Dr. Ed Murphy, in his book, *The Handbook for Spiritual Warfare* (1992), describes Satan's pattern of operation. First, the devil seeks to *deceive*. The primary deception is that we can do for ourselves and not need anyone else—especially God. Self-centeredness becomes the approach that many people take, leading to the hurting of others. Second, he targets *leaders*. If a solitary man sins, he alone may be affected, although a good argument can be made that no one is completely in solitude. If a family man sins, however, his entire family is affected. If a community leader sins, the entire community is affected. If a national leader sins, the entire nation is affected. Our own nation was mesmerized, and even immobilized for a time, when President Bill Clinton was caught in an affair with a young intern. If a world leader sins, the world itself can be affected. Such was the case with Adolf Hitler, for example. When church leaders fall due to immoral behaviors, as was the case with Jim Bakker/PTL, Ted Haggard in Colorado, and the many abuses of Catholic priests, it discredits the church of our God. This brings us to the third component, according to Dr. Murphy: namely, Satan's *purpose*. The devil's purpose is to bring dishonor to God, and everything about God, by bringing shame and harm to and through God's people.

We have seen over the last fifty years, an exponential increase in divorce, addictions, abuse of all kinds, and perversions among men and women, along with a growing sense of individualism—even within the church! The effect of such growing evils is the disintegration of the core longing of safety. Safety begins with one's relationship to God. Next, safety is to be present in families. The security of the family is the foundation of every healthy society. Fortunately, at the same time, there have been many efforts to strengthen the family through many churches, ministries and organizations, such as Focus on The Family, The Family Research Council, The American Family Association, and Promise Keepers, to name a few. These and many other ministries are helping to restore relationships within the family unit, thereby strengthening our own society.

I believe that the main thrust (and there are others, to be sure) of any effective family ministry, needs to focus on the man—the family leader; the husband and father; the priest of the home; the one who is responsible for the guidance, direction and even the outcome of the family. Now, before you consider me an over-the-top sexist or a male chauvinist, stay with me and hear my heart.

The man, as a husband and father, has been taking many hits over these changing times, through feminism, the media's portrayal of male roles in television shows and movies, reports of abuse and neglect on the part of men themselves, and the over exposure of homosexual behavior and the issues related to homosexuality. "There is much confusion today about the role of the father" (Vanier 2003). We hear that men cannot be trusted, that men are idiots, that men are brutes and that men need to tap into their "hidden feminine nature" in order for men to be effective and even accepted today. Most women want to be in a relationship with a man who is clear, strong, kind, knows where he is going, can stand up when confronted, and can make a woman feel protected and safe. They really don't have a lot of confidence in someone who is passive, unsure, and unwilling to fight the good fight when needed.

Men can be compassionate without losing their masculinity. "There is a trend today to suppress the differences between men and women" (Vanier 2003). I know of many men today who have actually stated to me that they want their woman to take care of them. That is selfish, lazy, and wrong. "Men are in danger of fleeing from their own vulnerability and capacity for tenderness. They seek a wife-mother and then, very quickly and like small boys, they reject her because they want their freedom" (Vanier 2003). I have found this to be true among many of our men today. Men want a mother, not necessarily a wife. The care for each other is to be reciprocal. Eventually, the man becomes resentful of the control he has allowed his wife to have over him, and in many cases, will leave and become entangled in another relationship that has the appearance of freedom. John Eldridge stated, "A man does not go to a woman to get his strength, he goes to offer it" (Eldridge 2001, 115).

What we are missing is the *complete* understanding of how God created the universe and the way He set up the chain of command, if you will. I believe that once we adopt God's way of conducting relationships and living responsibly, men *and* women, as well as the children in the homes, will embrace the benefits that come as a result. Unfortunately, this seems radical for our time and may come up against ridicule. While it is true that men are the priests of our homes, called to be leaders and providers, etc., I believe we need to see our roles more completely and more balanced than ever before. If that can be accomplished, I believe many will take notice and respond in positive ways. In his book, *Wild at Heart*, John Eldredge states, "God made men the way they are because we desperately need them to be the way they are" (Eldredge 2001, 83). I am speaking of the concept called *"covering"* which will be defined in Chapter 3. As men, we are called to cover! Cover what?—that for which we are *responsible*. In God's plan, that means first, we are to cover our wives and children. Our families need to know that they are safe: relationally safe; financially safe; emotionally safe; environmentally safe; and physically safe, just for starters.

Men, too, need to feel safe, and our relationship with God provides that. Many men feel God is a crutch—something or someone to lean on only when we are crippled and weak, to be tossed aside when we can do for ourselves. The Bible gives a great picture of God as our covering in Proverbs 18:10: "The name of the Lord is a strong tower; the righteous man runs into it and is safe." It is the righteous man, not the weak man, who runs to the Lord, knowing that as a strong tower, God will guard and guide with love and faithfulness. When someone feels safe, they can be creative, confident, relationally engaging, and at peace.

Then we are to cover our various responsibilities and relationships as employers, employees, managers, ministers, etc. Even as we are to discuss this, we as men cannot miss the fact that *we* are not without a covering. Scripture teaches clearly, than God Himself is man's covering, (1 Cor. 11:3). Gentlemen, we answer to the Big Guy! We always have to be accountable to Him regarding our hearts, our behavior, our effectiveness, and our calling.

Men, as you read this book, my prayer is that we can grow in our functioning as the covering to our families and in all for which we are responsible, as God designed. Women, my prayer is that you will be motivated to encourage your husband to be all he is called to be, for by doing so, it will actually benefit you beyond your dreams. Each husband and wife should be able to recognize the gift each truly is to the other. Children and families, my prayer is that you will experience the benefits of living under a proper and caring covering, in order for you to know the influence your family can have in the world around you.

Psalm 33:12 states, "Blessed is the nation whose God is the Lord." Our nation has experienced some embarrassing issues related to the leaders of our country. It seems like every week, some leader is caught in infidelity, financial crimes, sexual crimes, corruption, or dealing with hurtful addictions of some kind. These discoveries, among mostly men leaders, bring a bad reflection upon the man, the role he plays, his family, and the institution or our nation. If a man would simply walk under His covering, he then would be a much more effective covering for his family, and the progressive chain reaction would indeed occur over time. Look at the promise God made to Abraham: "I will make you a great *nation*,[emphasis mine] and I will bless you, and make your name great, and so you shall be a blessing" (Gen. 12:2); and to Moses: "I will make you a great *nation*"[emphasis mine] (Exod. 32:10).

God starts with a man; covers him; calls man to remain under His covering; calls men and women to be each a covering who is responsible, relational and reliable; calls parents, fathers and mothers, to cover their children; calls leaders to cover their responsibilities; calls us all to provide safe and secure environments, as best we can, to those who depend upon us. As a result, a man will have wonderful and loving wife, a great family, a positive influence, and even a nation may be his!

CHAPTER 1

In the Beginning—God's Design

Whenever I conduct a class as an adjunct professor, whether in our adult education program at church, at a seminar, or in a workshop at conferences, I typically like to start at the very beginning. While this may not be terribly profound, I do find that "the beginning" allows for a tremendous outlook on the original design. In many cases, Genesis, the book of beginnings, is such an excellent starting point. Throughout this biblical book, we see God's intention for His creation and for humankind in particular.

The Scriptures, both Old and New Testaments, are the unfolding of God's plan with and for humankind, which includes the purposes of men and women and their redemptions. However, once in a while, we are allowed glimpses of what takes place behind the scenes in the heavenly realms. These glimpses are ever so brief, so we must always understand them in light of the rest of Scripture. God's creation of the heavens and the earth is a case in point.

Throughout the centuries, from the ancient Israelites through Christianity today, creation has been held to be a foundational truth of faith in God. Today, it is hotly debated, even ridiculed, by science and those who believe in the theory of evolution. In addition, there are several views to the creation story itself that have found adherents throughout history. The scope of this book is not to delineate these various teachings about the creation story, but one prominent view will be briefly discussed, as I believe it relates to the understanding of the subject of this book—covering. It is called the Gap Theory, or as Dr. Barnhouse calls it, The Great Interval (1965).

Essentially, this doctrine teaches that there was an unknown span of time between Genesis 1:1 and Genesis 1:2, that God indeed created the heavens and the earth perfectly and with integrity, but then "reformed" the earth as a result of chaos and darkness that somehow developed on the earth after His initial creation. The Hebrew language lends credence to this possibility when the verb in verse 2 actually reads, "the earth *became* formless and void, and darkness was over the surface of the deep" (emphasis mine). The same Hebrew verb is used in Genesis 19:26 when it reads, "Lot's wife looked back and she *became* a pillar of salt" (emphasis mine). The word translated "formless" in Hebrew is *tohu*, which means "confusion," "chaos," and "waste" in several other places in Scripture. The word translated "void" in Hebrew is *bohu*, which means "emptiness." For some reason, the earth *became* a wreck and a ruin and filled with chaos and darkness.

Two other prominent places in the Old Testament use these same words—tohu and bohu. The first is Isaiah 45:18: "For thus says the Lord, who created the heavens (He is the God who formed the earth and made it, He established it and *did not create it a waste place* [italics added], but formed it to be inhabited)." The second passage is Jeremiah 4:23: "I looked on the earth, and behold, it was *formless and void* [italics added]; And to the heavens, and they had no light."

Much of the rest of this chapter of Jeremiah speaks of God's anger and judgment as to why the earth was in such a state. All throughout Scripture, wasteland or wilderness were typically depicted as places of evil or judgment.

The careful reader of the first chapter of Genesis will note that the Hebrew word for create, *bara*, is found in the first verse and appears no more in the account until the introduction of animal and human life in the fifth and sixth days of the restoration (Barnhouse, 1965). This word, *create*, means to produce out of nothing. The other words, which are used to describe the work of the six days, such as *made, divide, fashion*, and *set*, are used elsewhere in Scripture to describe the work done with existing materials (Barnhouse, 1965). This does not diminish the fact that God's word was the active force in creation. God still spoke, and by His word the necessary transformation and restoration was put in motion and completed. He is still the Creator. "For He spoke and it was done" (Ps. 33:9). God stated that what He did in restoring the earth was good and even very good (Gen. 1:4, 10, 12, 18, 21, 25). Adam's sin caused the earth to be cursed later.

We are not told how long this possible interval was, nor are we told the details of what constituted the creation of the earth. Some critics of the Gap Theory say that it includes prior inhabitants of the earth. However, the Scriptures never allude to this, and it is not necessary for it to be true in order to consider such a theory of creation. The earth's darkness and need of God's redemption could have simply been a result of the expulsion of Lucifer from heaven to the earth, as we will see below in the subsequent discussions of the Isaiah and Ezekiel passages. In these passages, it appears that God may have placed Lucifer as a *covering* over the earth, but his pride and arrogance destroyed his effectiveness.

In addition, it is highly noteworthy that God separated the darkness from the light before He began to restore His creation (Gen. 1:3–4). "God is light, and in Him there is no darkness at all" (1 John 1:5). Since there is no darkness in Him, the question is, where did darkness come from? Perhaps God has been in the redemption and restoration business longer than most of us may have believed since it appears He saved what was lost and brought light into the darkness from the very beginning.

Note that, while there is great debate regarding this theory, this explanation is not new. Indeed, it has been found in early church writings and scholarly works. Some of the early Reformers in Europe also held this belief. Gap creationism was popularized by Thomas Chalmers (1780–1847), a divinity professor at the University of Edinburgh, founder of the Free Church of Scotland, and author of one of the Bridgewater Treatises, who attributed the theory to seventeenth century Dutch Armenian theologian Simon Episcopius (1583–1643). Also, Canadian physiologist Arthur Custance has argued that the belief can be traced back to biblical times, citing the Targum of Onkelos (second century BC), Akiba ben Joseph's *Sefer Hazzohar* (first century AD), Origen's *De Principiis* (third century AD), and Caedmon (seventh century AD). Origen, incidentally, is considered by many to be the first theologian of the Christian faith.

Today, many resource books and commentaries discuss this as a viable explanation. Admittedly, Scripture only gives glimpses of behind-the-scenes scenarios. Even if the Gap Theory was not to be considered, we can still note the drastic effect of Lucifer's expulsion from heaven, and, as a result, his "covering" role dramatically changing forever. As the debate rages on, however, I believe this thought is viable enough for our discussion of covering.

So, what happened between Genesis 1:1 and 1:2? Perhaps nothing, or perhaps something terrible and catastrophic that caused chaos and waste in God's wonderful works!

Lucifer

When we see that, in the beginning, God created the heavens and the earth, and that He did not create them to be a waste place and a ruin, we come to a point at which we need to see that their corruption was a result of judgment. Judgment of what or of whom? I believe we are allowed another glimpse by virtue of some very important passages of Old Testament Scriptures.

Ezekiel 28:12–18:

> Thus says the Lord God, "You had the seal of perfection, full of wisdom, and perfect in beauty. You were in Eden, the garden of God; every precious stone was your covering: the ruby, the topaz, and the diamond; the beryl the onyx and the jasper; the lapis lazuli, the turquoise and the emerald; and the gold, the workmanship of your settings and sockets, was in you. On the day that you were created they were prepared. You were the anointed cherub who *covers*, and I placed you there. You were on the holy mountain of God; you walked in the midst of the stones of fire. You were blameless in your ways from the day you were created until unrighteousness was found in you. By the abundance of your trade you were internally filled with violence, and you sinned; Therefore I have cast you as profane from the mountain of God. And I have destroyed you, O *covering* cherub, from the midst of the stones of fire. Your heart was lifted up because of your beauty; You corrupted your wisdom by reason of your splendor. I cast you to the ground; I put you before kings, that they may see you. By the multitude of your iniquities, in the unrighteousness of your trade you profaned your sanctuaries.

Therefore I have brought fire from the midst of you; it has
consumed you, and I have turned you to ashes on the earth
in the eyes of all who see you" [emphasis added].

In this passage, we are given a behind-the-scenes narrative of
what took place in the heavenly realms. This "covering" cherub was
indeed beautiful and perfect, powerful, and given much responsibility
by God. It is very clear that this cherub was created and placed in
his position by God. This cherub was in Eden. This cherub served
in a priestly role of some kind by virtue of the fact that he evidently
had sanctuaries where he served as priest and worship leader of the
heavenly host.

The Old Testament high priests had special garments that
included a breastplate of twelve precious stones. Nine of those same
precious stones are described as being a part of this cherub's "covering."
These stones portray the priestly garment. The "mountain of God"
throughout Scripture is symbolic of the government of God. The
"stones of fire" portray the worship and presence of God almighty.
This cherub, perhaps the chief of all created beings, was set in the
government of God as the governor—or the "covering"—over the
creation of God, to guard it, protect it, and keep it safe.

Yet, because of his unrighteousness and corruption, this mighty
cherub profaned his sanctuaries and was cast from the presence of
God to the ground. His role as one who covers was removed. In fact,
that which he covered was adversely affected by his rebellion. This is
an important truth to consider throughout this book—that is, one's
pride and rebellion adversely affects one's ability to cover things for
which one is responsible.

Evidently, this was a violent exchange, indicated by the effect it
had upon the earth.

Revelation 12:3–4, 7–9 confirms this clearly:

> Then another sign appeared in heaven: and behold, a great dragon having seven heads and ten horns, and on these horns were seven diadems. And his tail swept away a third of the stars of heaven and threw them to the earth ... And there was war in heaven, Michael and his angels waging war with the dragon. The dragon and his angels waged war, and they were not strong enough, and there was no longer a place found for them in heaven. And the great dragon was thrown down, the serpent of old who is called the devil and Satan, who deceives the whole world; he was thrown down to the earth, and his angels were thrown down with him.

This violent exchange had a colossal effect upon the earth, bringing chaos and darkness upon it. This account does not refer to something yet future. Rather, it is describing that which has already occurred. The devil, because of his expulsion from heaven, now has negatively impacted the earth in drastic ways.

The second Old Testament passage helps us understand *why* this covering cherub was cast out of heaven to the earth, and it is found in Isaiah 14:12–17:

> How you have fallen from heaven, O star of the morning, son of the dawn! You have been cut down to the earth, you who have weakened the nations! But you said in your heart, "*I will* ascend to heaven; *I will* raise my throne above the star of God, and *I will* sit on the mount of assembly in the recesses of the north. *I will* ascend above the heights of the clouds; *I will* make myself like the Most High." Nevertheless, you will be thrust down to Sheol, to the recesses of the pit ... who shook kingdoms, who made the world like a wilderness [emphasis added].

It is from this passage that we obtain the name "Lucifer," a Latin word that means "star of the morning" or "light bearer." Lucifer was the angel of light, beautiful and glorious on the mountain of God, escorting all of creation into God's holy presence through worship and his priestly function and leadership. Iniquity was found in him, and this sin was that of pride in his role and in his beauty and a desire to be like God, in a way that would place him above the Almighty. When Lucifer declared that he wanted to ascend above "the heights of the clouds," this is to be understood as the "cloud" of God's glory. This covering cherub wanted to not only come out from under his covering, God Himself, but he also wanted to be his own covering, and to be more exalted than God. This sin of pride, independence and the rebellion that followed was what led to Lucifer's judgment and expulsion from heaven.

The origin of sin can be explained through this heavenly scenario, and by Ezekiel 28:15 especially, when Lucifer was said to have been created blameless, but then sometime in the beginning, unrighteousness was found in him.

> By his sin, he lost, of necessity, the office of prophet since God no longer could use this unholy one as the mouth-piece for divine decrees. By his sin, he lost the office of priest because he stole the worship, which was due to God alone and kept it for himself. Now we see that by his sin, he had lost the right of being God's steward and governing for God, Who says, "I have destroyed you, O covering cherub, from the midst of the stones of fire." (Barnhouse 1965, 35).

God created the heavens and the earth. Perhaps He placed Lucifer as the primary cherub in all of creation, giving him the responsibility of overseeing, or covering, the earth and the heavenly host, acting as heavenly priest and worship leader, bringing glory to God through his service and leadership. He was not left without a covering himself, as God almighty was still God over all His creation. God simply delegated much into the hands of Lucifer. However, Lucifer developed pride and unholy ambition, and God, who does not share His glory with anyone, relieved him of his high-ranking leadership. When Lucifer stepped out from under the covering, *his own covering ability was lost,* and the result was a catastrophic transformation of what he once covered. Chaos, formlessness, and darkness came upon the earth.

"And the Spirit of God was moving over the surface of the waters. Then God said, 'Let there be light,' and there was light. God saw that the light was good; and God *separated the light from the darkness* [emphasis added]" (Gen. 1:2–4). Perhaps this was the beginning of the Lord's restoration, as He brought light into the world again. God made it clear that under His rule, darkness could not exist and had to be separated from the light. Yet He desired to find a replacement for Lucifer as the governor or covering over the earth. Who was that going to be?

CHAPTER 2
Divine Delegation

Of all the vast and countless host of heaven, only three angels are ever identified by name in Scripture. These angels, evidently, had very specific roles assigned to them by God. The word *angel* simply means *messenger*, and as a whole, that is how God employs these spiritual beings. There appears to be a hierarchy among the heavenly host, as the Bible speaks of cherubim (Gen. 3:24; Ezek. 11:22), seraphim (Isa. 6:2, 6) and archangels (1 Thess. 4:16), all being delegated by God for a purpose.

We have already learned about *Lucifer*, the priest, worship leader, and covering cherub over God's creation. One of the other named angels is *Gabriel*, whose name means, "God's hero" or "mighty one." Gabriel is associated with the conveying and interpreting of divine revelations, specifically related to the coming Messiah and salvation of humankind (Dan. 8:16; Luke 1:19–26). God delegated Gabriel to be a mouthpiece of hope during times of gloom and discouragement.

The other named angel is *Michael*, whose name means, "who is like unto God?" References to him in the book of Daniel indicate that he is a "prince" among the angels, and the expression, "one of the chief princes" (Dan. 10:13) suggests ascending rank among angels (Leahy 1990). Michael is seen as a valiant and mighty angel, fighting against the powers of evil, and the enemies of God and of His people (Jude 9; Rev. 12:7).

With the entire heavenly host that God had at His disposal, He chose to pursue a very curious option. Genesis 1:26–28, 31:

> Then God said, "Let Us make man in Our image, according to Our likeness; and let them rule over the fish of the sea and over the birds of the sky and over the cattle and *over all the earth* [emphasis added] and over every creeping thing that creeps on the earth." God created man in His own image, in the image of God He created him; male and female He created them. God blessed them; and God said to them, "Be fruitful and multiply, and fill the earth, and subdue it; and rule over the fish of the sea and over the birds of the sky and *over every living thing that moves on the earth*" [emphasis added] ... God saw all that He had made, and behold, it was very good.

God created man, or more accurately, humankind, which includes male *and* female, to rule over the earth, the fish, birds, and beasts and to have a growing dominion as man multiplied. The inference here is that human beings were to cover the earth with a responsible and a righteous rule and dominion. The Bible is also clear to say that God placed humankind in Eden (Gen. 2:8), to cultivate it and keep it (Gen. 1:15).

The Garden of Eden was a real place, and was to be a place where the presence of God dwelt, for God walked in the "garden in the cool of the day" (Gen. 3:8). It was here that God always chose to converse with Adam and Eve, and for them to hear from their Father. Their relationship was open and safe. He walked with them, and talked with them, just as Charles Austin Miles wrote in 1912 in the old hymn, "In the Garden."

The Scriptures are also clear that God dealt directly with Adam. Even though God called male *and* female to take dominion over creation together as a partnership, God singled Adam out for a reason. It is clear that Adam spent an unknown amount of time on earth before Eve came along. During this time, it would be reasonable to believe that God instructed Adam regarding his call, his responsibility, and the blessings that are a part of having such a relationship with the Creator Himself. The Lord, perhaps, spent much time imparting to Adam all that was needed to represent and reflect God throughout all of creation. God even brought all the creatures to Adam to name. By naming all the animals, God was confirming to Adam his leadership and dominion over them. When someone has the ability to name something else, such a position also indicates that the one who names provides a level of responsibility, guidance, and care over that which was named. This is true of parents, business founders, and church planters, to name a few. This daunting task also showed Adam that he was to be the covering over the earth, because no one else was given this responsibility; not even the angels.

Take a look at Psalms 8:3–9:

> When I consider Your heavens, the work of Your fingers, the moon and the stars, which You have ordained; What is man that You take thought of him, and the son of man that You care for him? Yet You have made him a little lower than God, and you crown him with glory and majesty! You *make him to rule over the works of Your hands; You have put all things under his feet,* [italics added] all sheep and oxen, and also the beasts of the field, the birds of the heavens and the fish of the sea, whatever passes through

the paths of the seas. O Lord, our Lord, how majestic is
Your name in all the earth.

Notice how it is clear, both in this passage, as well as in Genesis 2:8 that it was the Lord God who placed man in the position (dominion) and in the place (Eden), in which he found himself to be. God owns everything. God is over man and is man's covering. God *delegated* to man, the place and the purpose in which he needed to function and be effective. Man was to operate under total delegated freedom to oversee, or cover, what God gave him to do. What an awesome concept, if we really think about it! As in the workplace, men are to be stewards of that which belongs to someone else. Even if a man operates his own business, there are laws by which to operate in order to conduct business properly. Ultimately, however, any business owner has God as his covering.

When God delegated to man the awesome responsibility of the earth, He not only coached and taught him what he needed to know, but gave Adam everything he needed to be sustained. God trained Adam to be competent and provided Adam with what he needed to succeed. Every tree of the Garden was good for food, and God directed man to be free to eat from any tree, except one. In fact, Genesis 2:5–8 indicates that God did not even create the plants or shrubs, until He was about to create man, so that man could be the covering and nurturer over this part of creation. "No shrub of the field was yet in the earth ... there was no man to cultivate the ground" (v. 5). The connotation was God had man in mind when He designed creation.

Part of delegating to someone often means that the "delegator" grants access to much of his enterprise, yet still retaining ownership and having the prerogative to maintain certain other important areas.

When I served as a manager of a local retail store for ten years, within a chain of over 200 stores nationwide, I had the responsibility for that store. I could hire and fire, set the schedule, and monitor the sales figures and budget to my store. However, I did not have responsibility for any of the other stores, nor their staffs, nor their sales figures. I was the covering for my store alone. The district manager was my covering; the area sales manager was his covering, and so on up the corporate ladder. A store manager could have the opportunity to be promoted to a district manager, provided he or she showed success, followed company policies, kept the company assets safe, and remained responsible for his or her local store. In such cases, they would then have access to more information, have more responsibility, and be a covering for more than just one store. This honor came with faithfulness proven over time.

Jesus taught a parable of the talents in Matthew 25:14–30. In this parable, two of the workers saw their efforts and investments grow because of their responsible behavior, while the other worker, gained nothing for his very little effort. The first two individuals were good stewards and provided good "covering" over what was given them. Jesus summarized in verse 29, "For to everyone who has, more will be given, and he will have an abundance." While at first glance this may seem unfair, but Jesus was speaking of the concept of being a *responsible* steward. Keeping things, and people, safe and secure will lead to growth and increase. God gives increase to those who are faithful at managing little (Matt. 25:23). This concept continues to be true in the marketplace. However, it began as a kingdom concept.

God did a similar thing with Adam by commanding him not to eat from the tree of the knowledge of good and evil. Over time, Adam had the knowledge he needed to respond responsibly. It was when Adam went beyond what God decreed to him and gave to him, that things went awry. Yet God's desire was for Adam to be fruitful and to multiply, but it was never to be without his dependence upon God. Remember, it was Lucifer's desire to be self-oriented that lead to his demise. When we stay within the bounds of what is delegated, yet showing initiative and responsibility, we can be sure to see our tents expanded. God is the "delegator" and the "orchestrator." Gentlemen, we have been given many things to cover, such as our wife, children, our vocational responsibilities, and ministries, for example. Yet please let us not forget that we are not without our own covering—that of the Owner and "Great Delegator." We are not an army of one. More could be given to any responsible and faithful steward, but that comes as we serve with integrity and with honor. Men cannot be effective leaders unless they are at the same time, surrendered subordinates.

CHAPTER 3
Covering for Men

The concept of covering can be also expressed by the term "headship," but many might recoil at this term. The idea of submission is also a chronic conflict within the church and society. This will be discussed further in chapter four, but suffice it to say at this point that true headship has to do strictly with *function* and *responsibility*. Even though there is unity in the Trinity, God the Father, the Son, and the Holy Spirit express themselves through different functions. The same is true of the oneness in marriage. The husband and wife are one, but they are designed for and called to different functions. This concept is not to deter us from the truth that men and women are *equal* in value and worth, and are both to be treated with love, honor, and understanding. Both husband and wife desire safety in the relationship and in the home. God does not value men more than he values women. God did not feel that males were somehow nobler or less sinful than females (Baker 1991). In fact, we have seen that sin and death entered the human generations through the man (Baker 2001).

Nevertheless, marriage and gender roles *are* in conflict, and this issue, according to Beck (2000), is one that is largely overlooked, even within the church. He correctly argues that this is an important question for Christian counselors, educators and researchers, though we have not yet acknowledged it as such. The "headship" position, along with the contrasting "egalitarian" position, has been seen as too polarizing within Scriptural understanding. The headship position often touts men as "superior" to women, which is *not* Scriptural. The egalitarian view, on the other hand, has a husband and wife operating separately from each other, to the point where independence from one another exists. Ohlschlager and Hawkins (2001), through their experience and research, have found that both headship and egalitarian positions devolve into something far less than what we now believe God is seeking in marriage.

For men, I believe our role or function is more accurately expressed through the idea of covering, as it conveys more closely the model that Jesus provides and what Scripture teaches. Jesus' example conveys more of a "servant–leader" approach. Leaders "can only command if we know how to obey. We can only be a leader if we know how to be a servant" (Vanier 2003). The Son of God always remained under the covering of the Father, yet He would operate with great power and freedom and later delegate to His disciples certain areas of ministry. The same is true for men. Men are *responsible* for the outcome, while not needed always to be "in charge." This is the essence of *covering*. Covering is leadership *within* a family or group. The place where the "buck stops," is a position of function, not superiority.

Husbands and wives can and should collaborate and serve each other, but I believe that God will approach the man directly and ultimately hold him responsible for the outcome of whatever he covers. Why? Because a man is not without a covering and he is called to be submissive to the Father. This is a challenge for men, since as leaders, we often forget that we are not "lone rangers."

Allow me to define "covering" at this point. A dictionary will render several concepts of covering, all of which aptly describe this truth. According to Webster's dictionary, to cover means *to place something (or someone) upon or over as to protect, guard, defend, or shield from harm, loss, or danger.* Safety! It also can mean *to clothe,* as God did when He covered Adam and Eve with the skins of an animal (Gen. 3:21). Another synonym is *to substitute for,* as if a substitute teacher would say, "I will cover her class," until the teacher returns. As mentioned earlier, we are stewards of God's creation, as if we are substitutes for Him, while we are waiting for Him to return.

The apostle Paul writes in 1 Corinthians 11:3, "But I want you to understand that Christ is the head of every man, and the man is the head of every woman, and God is the Head of Christ." As long as Adam obeyed and followed God, he was under God's covering and influence. However, once Adam succumbed to Satan's deception and ate of the forbidden tree, Adam stepped out from under God's covering. Once Adam moved out from under God's covering, he knew that he sinned and saw that he was naked. Then *he hid from* God. In other words, in his attempt to hide, Adam sought out another "covering"—to cover himself *from* God, rather than be covered *by* God!

In Scripture, nakedness can denote shame. Nakedness, whether it be physically or spiritually, literally occurs when covering is gone. In practical terms, we are the most vulnerable, or unsafe, when we are naked. Yet God was quick to act in His grace, by slaying an animal, and covering, (re-covering?) Adam and Eve with the skins of the sacrificed animal (Gen. 3:21), symbolizing the need from that point on, for the restoration of a covering, through the shedding of blood.

A substitute's blood had to be shed in order to provide the covering that men and women need to overcome guilt and shame. Since Christ provided the ultimate sacrifice, He is man's covering, or perhaps more accurately, man's "recovering."

Men, even as leaders, we are to be under submission. Notice, if you will, the fact that God *called for Adam*, when they tried to hide themselves, and not for Eve (Gen. 3:9). Adam was directly accountable to God. It is *never* called "Eve's sin" in Scripture, but it is stated that Adam sinned (Rom. 5:14). Why is that? Let's look at Genesis 3:6:

> When the woman saw that the tree was good for food, and that it was a delight to the eyes, and that the tree was desirable to make one wise, she took from its fruit and ate; and she gave also to her husband *with her* [italics added] and he ate.

The actual Hebrew reads that Adam was *with* her during this entire time! While it is true that Eve was *deceived* (2 Cor. 11:3, 1 Tim. 2:14), Adam was held responsible by God as Eve's covering, for the disobedience, since he knew the instructions of God. Adam did not protect his wife from falsehood and harm. He did not keep her, or the truth about God, safe!

I have often wondered, where we all would be today, if Adam had protected his family and simply stood firm against the serpent and said something like this: "Get thee behind me Satan! This is *not* what my Father has said." In that moment, at least, I believe Adam's responsible covering leadership would have solidified his dominion, and would have prevented sin and shame from contaminating humankind. Did not Jesus do something similar when Peter pleaded to Him that He was not to die? Jesus responded to Peter's rebuke by saying, "Get behind Me, Satan: for you are not setting your mind on God's interests, but man's" (Matt. 16:23). If Adam had recognized that the serpent was suggesting something that was not in God's interest, and then responded accordingly, I believe things in the Garden would have been very different as result.

Gentlemen, in whatever we do, we will eventually have to be accountable to God. Ladies, if your husband abides under God's covering, and *submits* to Him, then you are truly blessed, and your submission to him is not a dirty word. We all need to remember, that anything in God's original design was completed with purpose, with integrity and was seen as good or very good.

Ever since the original fall, the blame game has existed. Men will readily place the blame on their wives for issues related to anything from bad financial decisions to the wrong colored tie he chose to wear. Women will also be quick to blame their husbands, but their discussions can be more like guerilla warfare. Women will often blame and undermine their husbands while they visit with their girlfriends, or to anyone who will listen, while men are often more direct to their wives in their accusations. Both tactics will torpedo the primary needs of each—to feel safe in the relationship. A woman will feel unloved when her man blames her, while the man often feels dishonored or disrespected when he believes that their "dirty laundry," has been broadcast to the general population. Usually, within a given conflict, both are "to blame" even if it is at varying degrees. God's way would be for both to seek forgiveness from each other, receive grace from each other, and partner together towards a plan of action. This approach is underscored by 1 Peter 4:8: "Love *covers* [italics added] a multitude of sins."

Covering incorporates several important aspects. The purpose and benefits of covering exist for both men and women. For men, covering provides *purpose, responsibility, guidance,* and *protection.* With a right attitude and a right relationship with God, covering for men can be empowering. Psalms 128:1–6 says:

> How blessed is everyone who fears the Lord, who walks in His ways. When you shall eat of the fruit of your hands, you will be happy and it will be well with you. Your wife shall be like a fruitful vine within your house, your children like olive plants around your table. Behold, for thus shall the man be blessed who fears the Lord. The Lord bless you from Zion, and may you see the prosperity of Jerusalem all the days of your life. Indeed, may you see your children's children. Peace upon Israel!

This passage is obviously addressing the man, with promises for the man who fears God. If the man is a good "coverer," he will enjoy the fruit of his own hands, and not be stealing from others. He will see a wife who is respectful, (a *fruitful* vine), and not bitter. His children will be like "olive plants." Olive plants and trees can only flourish if watered and cultivated. Olive branches also denote peace. They need focused attention and care. When the father does the same to his children, they will in turn flourish in the way they were taught. Also, peace in the home is every man's dream, but it takes both surrender to God and attentiveness to his purpose and responsibility, in order for him to experience it. Peace is not the *absence* of conflict, but rather the *knowledge* of Who is in control when overcoming conflict!

Purpose

From the beginning, God set man to cover His earth, both with offspring and with rulership. God's agenda was to accomplish much through the righteous seed of man. Man's purpose was to bring glory to God, through his service, obedience, and worship, and to have an impact in all that he does. More will be said about this in my book, *Created for Purpose*. The book, *The Purpose Driven Life*, by Rick Warren, was a best seller because many adults and children are lacking a sense of purpose. We have experienced many distractions, evil occurrences, and fear that immobilize us today in our society, not unlike many men of the Old Testament.

Moses, for example, was called to be a deliverer of God's people in Egypt. In Exodus 3:7 through Exodus 4:14, we see how God established His purpose for Moses by calling him to be the deliverer. However, because of fear, Moses tried to avoid his purpose. Moses argued with God five times, but God was persistent, and Moses eventually followed through. He was prevented from reaching the promised land, however, because of his disobedience later in his journey. Had Moses trusted God's covering over him, he might have experienced all God had for him.

David was called to be King of Israel while just a young lad (1 Sam. 16:12–13) and was very successful in his endeavors. God's purpose was for David to rule with a righteous hand, and expand the kingdom. While he was king, David experienced success after success and peace for all his people. Then one day, while he was not with his military as he was supposed to be, he became distracted by Bathsheba's beauty and lusted after her. He committed adultery, then murder, to try and cover up his sin, but he was eventually discovered (2 Sam. 11, 12). From this point on, David experienced death of his children, incest among his children, violence in his home, and war in the land. Once David came out from under God's covering, because of sin, his purpose was altered tremendously and as a result, his house operated in chaos.

I have spent many hours with men who have experienced evil

in their lives, have chosen to turn their backs on what they know to be right, and who experienced a lack of affirmation of purpose for their lives. These men often go through life with anger, addictions, and lack of commitment, which, in turn, affect those around them in negative ways. I have found that wives who come to counseling typically are not looking to leave their husbands. Instead, they are often crying out for safety in their relationship and for their husbands to change and be all that they need to be. This is a high calling for men to serve God in what they have been given. In particular, for me, the first measure of my success in life is how my family is and how they turn out. Success in any other arena is not even a close second.

Responsibility

As Adam's covering, God was responsible for instructing him in the way he was to go and then providing him with what was needed to get there. The Scriptures show that God called man to take dominion. Then he showed man the provisions to sustain his efforts (Gen. 1:28–29). God also brought all the animals and birds to man, and gave him the responsibility to name every one of them (Gen. 2:19). Possessing the power to name something or someone denotes responsibility for, or guardianship over, those being named. For example, besides all the animals, Adam also named Eve (Gen. 3:20). Often, God chose to change the names of several people in the Bible, all to denote a changed purpose for their lives and a renewed responsibility. One example would be, Jacob (supplanter) to Israel (prince with God), (Gen. 32:24–32).

In like manner, a man is held responsible to train those he is guardian over, mainly his family. One of the most common mistakes men and women make today is that they want to be their child's friend, not their parents. Because of the fear of rejection, men would rather not confront or discipline their child. Often, they may even pass the role of being "the heavy" onto their wives. The father may have to make difficult stands with their child, but in the end, that will have a higher return. A child can always find friends, but he or she will only have one father (I Cor. 4:15).

We train by example (Ps. 101:2–4), by direct instruction (Deut. 4:9–10), and by loving discipline (Prov. 13:24). Among the things children learn from their parents, their dads in particular, are: (1) attitudes and values, (2) how to respond or react to challenges in life, (3) how to respond to various life situations, (4) how to respond in the marketplace (business ethics), and (5) how parents respond to each other. How we treat our wives is especially poignant, because we model how to be "coverings" and how to respect women. Values are caught before they are taught.

Men, we are the *primary* models to our children, and as such, we carry an awesome amount of power and influence. Do you ever allow your children to see you when you experience a failure or a sorrow? Have they ever seen you cry? Then can you say that they have seen you recover in ways that show integrity and honor to God? We live a lie in our society that says failure and sorrow are automatic signs of weakness. We all have experienced failures and sorrows, but what we have not learned very well is how to *recover* from these disappointments. True strength is strength of spirit and character, and our kids, our families, the marketplace, our society, and our world are all looking for individuals who possess such qualities. However, this can only come from the strength and power that our covering—God Himself—provides for us and in us as we walk in relationship with Him.

We are also responsible for providing for those in our care. Provision for one's family includes more than food, clothing, and housing. We are to provide in all areas of life including spiritual, emotional, social, intellectual, vocational, and moral areas (Iverson 1979). Providing for our families is essentially bringing safety to our families. This can be difficult to see, as our country has become a nation where many fathers are absent. The United States, for example, leads the world in fatherless families (Burns & Scott 1994). There are approximately twenty-four million children, or 34 percent of all kids in the U.S., living in fatherless homes (Horn & Sylvester 2002). The number of children raised by single mothers more than tripled between 1960 and 2000 (U.S. Census Bureau, 2001). These are families without a God-designed covering, and we have seen, as a nation, an increase in crime, school dropout rates, substance abuse, and addictions, just to name a few. I believe there is a correlation. When Satan has been successful in "taking out" the covering, through whatever means, the family becomes vulnerable and susceptible to many evils. When the coverer comes out from under his covering, and abuses or neglects his authority, the family also is adversely affected. More about this will be discussed in chapter 6.

The model we provide through our adult relationships speaks much louder than words, especially as it relates to the treatment of others, principles that we live by, the respect for authority positions, and general values. For example, if we as men are not honoring those in authority over us (including God), then we will surely see our wives and children dishonor *us* as well.

Guidance

Many men today do not have the relationships with their children that are necessary to pass important characteristics on to them. This is mainly due to vocational pursuits, immaturity in themselves, and self-centeredness. Unfortunately, many parents are willing to sit back and let their children make their own decisions and find their own ways through life. Such a philosophy does not provide a sense of safety as a youngster grows up. The fact is, all of us need guidance, and we make decisions based upon what is imparted into our lives. Somewhere, our children will discover their values and base their decisions upon them, and it is God's design that parents become deliberate and proactive in imparting the guidance and tools children need to mature. Safety allows children to learn, make mistakes, and move on. Safety can reduce anxiety, which exists when an individual has difficulty making decisions in his or her life, fearing the worst. This is not to say we should always make decisions for our children; however, we are the primary resource for guidance and wisdom from which our kids make decisions.

I have known several parents over the years who have declared to me that they will not teach their children any one faith or any one set of values over another. Rather, they chose to let their kids decide for themselves. The outcome? In every case that I personally know, the children, who are now adults, do not have faith-filled lives; they have no respect for things of God and live by situational ethics. We will see in chapter 6 and 7 how God holds the *man* accountable for the outcome of his family.

When Abraham was called, God declared in Genesis 18:19: "For I have chosen him, so that he may command his children and his household after him to keep the way of the Lord by doing righteousness and justice, so that the Lord may bring upon Abraham what He has spoken about him." Part of the benefits of the covering is to see promises and purposes fulfilled in the lives of our children. If we stay under the covering of God, we will see the purposes and promises fulfilled in our lives. Then our responsibility is to impart to our children the proper training and attitudes for them to successfully find their purpose in life. Ephesians 6:4 says, "Fathers, do not provoke your children to anger, but bring them up in the discipline and instruction of the Lord."

Today, however, good parents do experience an increase in rebellion and challenge among their children. Young people are choosing more and more to disrespect their parents and to come out from under their covering. Cartoons and most movies, video games, and television shows portray an increasing cynical attitude towards parents and authority figures. This is to the detriment of the young person. Paul writes in Ephesians 6:1–3 that honoring your father and mother is the first commandment with promise, and if a child does so, things would go well with them. Children are never too old to honor their parents. If we want things to go well for us, then how we respond to our parents is key. We can readily admit that God knows more than we do. However, it is often ignored that parents know more than their children, even adult children. Parents have lived more life than their children, have gained more perspective and wisdom than their children, and we would be hurting ourselves when we dishonor the covering that our parents represent.

Parents do not feel the support for their Christian values that existed more than a generation ago. There are many reasons for this. Families have many outside forces that undermine proper respect, attentiveness, care, and protection. Fathers and mothers have to work much harder today, to have the influence on their children, than in the past. Biblical values and work ethics are increasingly missing from our society today. In the name of "progressiveness," we have seen the reduction of absolutes that provide safety and care. Independence is the idol of worship today. One of the results is a decrease in the safety and consideration of others. As long as we meet our own needs, so the current mindset declares, life is good.

Today's parents are more distracted than in the past, as well. There is more to be concerned with than when life was much simpler. The tendency is to take unsafe risks in order to stay ahead. We need to depend on our covering all the more, and to remain consistent and steady through the storms. Risks may be necessary indeed, but it is critical to know that God is leading us and will guide us through them. Consistency and dependability will always be sought out and embraced eventually. Our God is faithful, and He remains the same "yesterday, today, and forever" (Heb. 13:8).

One excellent resource is the book, *The Gift of The Blessing*, by Gary Smalley and John Trent (1993). This book outlines five ways to impart to our children the guidance necessary for their futures. The five ways are (1) meaningful touch, (2) a spoken message, (3) attaching high value to the one being blessed, (4) picturing a special future to the one being blessed and (5) an active commitment to fulfill the blessing. In Scripture, the model is that the father is the one who imparts such affirmation, as shown, for example, by Jacob in chapters 48 and 49 of Genesis. Jacob took the time to impart a special, indeed a prophetic, pronouncement of blessing upon each of his sons before he died. If a man is struggling in his own life regarding the blessing, then he may need to consider Christian counseling and receive a touch from God the Father. We can only impart that which we possess. Today, our children are crying out for direction, purpose and "the blessing."

Protection

Protection is one aspect of covering that is often overlooked or even despised. If we consider that God commanded Adam and Eve to avoid the tree of the knowledge of good and evil to *protect* them rather than withhold from them, an entirely new perspective occurs. Staying within restraints goes against our concept of freedom.

However, freedom is not the same as independence. Independence is doing whatever we want. Freedom is the power to do what is right. Our selfish desires for independence often lead us out of safety into danger and harm. It is amazing to me how often individuals deliberately participate in dangerous behavior, then wonder why they have injuries, illnesses, and problems as a result. Many times, I have had individuals blame God for their problems, when instead they chose to come out from under God's covering, or a covering in general.

When parents issue a curfew, for example, often the teenager views it as a hindrance to his or her freedom. In reality, most of the time, parents are simply looking to protect their children. My wife has often said over the years, "nothing good occurs after midnight." That is not far from the truth. When a young person criticizes, dishonors, or disrespects his or her parents, they are essentially devaluing the covering. Some common results of such actions to the young person are anxiety, nightmares, and anger issues. If the young person underestimates the value of parental protection, he or she will usually experience the consequence. The benefit of the covering for our sons, daughters, and women, in our present time, is especially to be considered with care.

For men, our heavenly Father desires to provide the covering in our lives. In my mind, if indeed I am accountable directly to God, I have found it truly behooves me to consider the ways of the Lord. Psalms 32:7 says, "You are my hiding place; You preserve me from trouble; You surround me with songs of deliverance." Also Psalm 119:114, "You are my hiding place and my shield; I wait for Your word." Knowing God's Word in our lives truly provides guidance and instruction. It is also true that as we live it, we will see the hand of the Lord around about us.

Our culture likes to say, "He's his own man." Depending on someone else is considered a sign of weakness. If we are honest with ourselves, *we are weak*, and in need of a Savior. Men, we need to be lead to "the rock that is higher than I" (Ps. 61:2). God's word does give us a tremendous promise: "I can do all things through Him who strengthens me" (Phil. 4:13). In reality, then, depending on God, our covering, actually sets us in places of strength.

An important truth to remember: If I walk in a way that keeps me under God's covering, then all those who are under my covering will, in turn, benefit as well. When Satan spoke to God about Job, he declared, "Have You not made a hedge about him and his house and all that he has, on every side? You have blessed the work of his hands, and his possessions have increased in the land" (Job 1:10). God did not deny this. In fact, Job was described as a man who was "blameless, upright, fearing God, and *turning away* from evil" [emphasis mine] (Job 1:1). God Himself described Job in a similar way to Satan in verse 8: "For there is no one like him on the earth, a blameless and upright man, fearing God and turning away from evil." Job was a righteous man, under God's covering, with a hedge of protection around his family and possessions, and enjoying increase in his influence. This can be true for *any man* today who is willing to be a man under authority and under God's protective covering. I believe we all underestimate the benefit of being "hedged in" by God. It is a place of safety and peace.

Now most of us know that Job suffered through devastating disappointment and pain, even though what God said about him was true. The devil had a field day destroying Job's possessions and family. Yet there was nothing to indicate that Job did anything to breach the hedge around his household. This may be true with many other families. Let's face it, we all live in a fallen world, with unforeseen situations that arrive at our doorsteps. Life can still have a way of bringing about unexpected hurts and rocking our world. Financial loss, medical conditions, traumatic and painful events, and more can have a devastating effect upon our lives. Yet God is still our covering through the difficult times. Job's attitude of disputing God did change in the end when he realized that God was still his covering and was able to restore what the devil had destroyed. After God addressed Job, "Now gird up your loins like a man ...," and reminded Job of His eternal eminence and goodness, Job's submission to his covering only became stronger. Job's reply is found in Job 40:1–5 and Job 42:1–6. Job's confession was that God could do all things, that His purposes would not be thwarted, and that he needed deeper understanding of God's love and His ways. In the end, God restored to Job ten children, and his possessions were restored two-fold.

Finally, we can learn much from the military. After all, we are all in a war—a spiritual war. The military is designed to prepare individuals for war. Its chain of command has two major purposes: order and protection. Soldiers are trained in discipline and how to "watch each other's back." Without order, chaos exists. In a scene from the movie, *The Patriot*, which was directed by Roland Emmerich and release by Columbia Pictures in June of 2000, General Cornwallis of the British army, was debating the rules of war with Colonel Benjamin Martin, the leader of the Colonial Militia. General Cornwallis was appealing to Col. Martin not to target the officers during battle. He described such tactics as being ungentlemanly and the cause of chaos among the soldiers should they see their commander fall. Leaders are responsible for order and protection among their troops and for making good strategic decisions for successful warfare in order to minimize casualties.

There is a clear understanding of responsibility, authority, and covering in the military. This helps explain the response Jesus had regarding the centurion in Matthew 8:5–13. This military leader came to Jesus, sharing with Him that his servant was home ill and under torment. Jesus offered to go to the centurion's home, but the soldier said:

> Lord, I am not worthy for You to come under my roof, but just say the word, and my servant will be healed. For I also am a man under authority, with soldiers under me; and I say to this one, 'Go!' and he goes, and to another, 'Come!' and he comes, and to my slave, 'Do this!' and he does it (v. 8–9).

Jesus marveled at this humble response and declared a very curious thing: "Truly I say to you, I have not found such *great faith* [italics added] with anyone in Israel" (v. 10). This Roman soldier understood trustworthy authority, and he surely recognized Jesus' authority. It was his faith in this authority to which Jesus responded. To walk under the authority or covering takes faith in that individual who is doing the covering.

Gentlemen, is your faith in God such that you follow Him? Is He worthy of our devotion? Absolutely! Ladies, is your faith such that you can follow your man, and in turn, follow God? Is your man worthy of devotion? Well, stay with me as we progress through the next few chapters and hopefully learn the answer to these questions.

CHAPTER 4

Covering for Women

The Bible says, "Therefore shall a man leave his father and mother, and shall cleave unto his wife; and they shall become one flesh" (Gen. 2:24, KJV). Being involved in many weddings over the years and premarital counseling, I have often heard this verse quoted and discussed. For a long time, however, the wording used in this statement would cause me to wonder: Since men *and* women leave their fathers and mothers, why is it that God chose to describe marriage as he did? Well, it dawned on me many years ago that God was describing the dynamics of a marriage relationship in such a way that reveals the *roles* as well as the concept of commitment.

First, for a man to leave his father and mother, he would have to be self-sustaining. The parents have been responsible *for him* while he was growing up. If the parents were doing their job properly, the young man would be ready to be *responsible for himself* in such a way that he could also be *responsible* for a future wife and family as well. A man is called to provide safety and security for his family and responsibilities. Essentially, we as parents are not raising children—we are raising *adults!* The issue is, is he ready to take care of whoever and whatever comes his way, or is he still looking to be taken care of? In her article, "It's Time to Grow Up – Later", dated September 30, 2004, Sharon Jayson of the USA Today newspaper cited a published study by the American Sociological Association that discovered in 1960, 65 percent of men and 77 percent of women had left home by age thirty, compared to 2004, where 31 percent of men and 46 percent of women had left home by age thirty. The reasons were related to readiness, maturity, and finances. This study did not take into account children who left home, only to return later. In God's design, when a man leaves his home, he should be ready to care for his own home!

For an unknown period, Adam was responsible for caring for God's creation on earth. He and Eve later formed a great partnership in stewardship. It can be safely implied that God spent time with Adam as He prepared him to care for His creation. God remained active through *relationship* with Adam, but Adam "was the man" on earth. Scripture indicates that God's plan was not to have Adam work alone, for God said, "It is not good for man to be alone; I will make him a helper suitable for him" (Gen. 2:18). The Hebrew word for "helper" in this verse is also found in several other places. Psalms 33:20—"Our soul waits for the Lord; He is our *help* and our shield." Also, Psalm 46:1—"God is our refuge and strength, a very present *help* in trouble." Finally, Psalms 63:7—"For you have been my *help* ..." (Italics added in each case.) This common word does not describe someone inferior, weak, lower, or less able. If that were so, then God would be described in such a way, as well. When God said He would make Adam a "helper," He meant someone who would aid and support him where he was weak (Littleton 1988). Eve was to be Adam's counterpart and equal partner. Adam was to be responsible for her, care for her, but he was also to be complete in her!

The second part of this passage from Genesis 2:24, indicates man's covering for his wife. The word *cleave* in Hebrew is *dabaq,* and it means, to "cling to," "adhere to," "be joined together with," and "keep." The idea here is to stick to someone with affection and loyalty. Man was to be joined to his wife in such a way as to provide her with love and security, every woman's primary needs. Becoming "one flesh" simply underscores this concept in Scripture, giving the word picture that a wife is secure in her husband, and the husband is fulfilled in his wife. Ephesians 5:28–29 underscores this truth: "So husbands ought also to love their own wives as their own bodies. He who loves his own wife loves himself; for no one ever hated his own flesh, but nourishes and cherishes it, just as Christ also does the church."

Throughout history and across many cultures, it is common and proper for a young man to seek permission from the father of the young woman for her hand in marriage. It has been proper to ask permission even to court the young woman. Once again, the movie, *The Patriot,* provides a good example of this tradition. Gabriel Martin develops an attraction to a young woman by the name of Anne Howard. He approaches her father and asks if he might write to her while away fighting with the militia. Mr. Howard grants him permission to do so. Later, he returns from several battles and asks Mr. Howard if he might "call on" Anne, and again, he grants permission. This was very common for the young man to gain permission from the father to pursue the daughter. The girl's covering, the father, was responsible to discern and determine with whom he could trust his daughter. This is true when the daughter is highly valued by the father. However, in our society today, young women often make the mistake of not considering the protection of their fathers. Or, the father is absent, not providing such safety or protection for his daughter.

The biblical story of Jacob is one of several in the Scriptures that convey a similar truth. In Genesis chapter 29, Jacob meets Rachel, falls in love with her, and asks her father, Laban, for her hand in marriage. Laban's response is, "It is better that I *give her to you* [italics added] than to give her to another man ..." (v. 19). So Jacob agrees to work seven years for Laban, in order to marry Rachel. Laban, the story goes, deceives Jacob and gives him Rachel's sister, Leah, to be his wife. When Jacob realizes he was duped, he agrees to serve Laban seven more years, for Rachel, who Laban granted Jacob in the end. For our purposes, this clearly illustrates the concept of a woman being covered, and the young man's respect for that covering, even if Laban was dishonest in his promise to Jacob. The man was to respect the woman's covering, namely her father, while the woman was to respect her own covering.

I have found, in counseling, that when a woman disrespects and seeks independence from the covering that her father provides, she often finds herself in some kind of distress and later treats her covering, which is her husband, in similar ways. There may be legitimate reasons for the young woman to leave her home, however, such as neglect and abuse, and we will discuss those in chapter 6. In the same way, if the young man disrespects the young woman's covering, he will often eventually disrespect his own wife and be very lacking in his own responsibility.

When one of my sons was a teenager, he was attracted to a young woman, who came from a good Christian family. The young woman was very interested in dating my son, but her parents stipulated that she could not date until she was at least sixteen years old. My son asked me what I thought about the situation, and my advice to him was to honor the wishes of the girl's father, who was her covering. Despite my son's feelings and the girl's desire to date against her father's wishes, my son chose to honor the covering. While my son and this young woman never did date later on, my son gained the respect of her parents, which remains today. My son has gone on to be a leader in his spheres of influence, mainly because he learned the power of honoring those in authority. As for the young woman, she is now married to a fine young man. This young man also respected her covering by seeking the father's permission for the young woman's hand in marriage. Today, they are married and serve as missionaries overseas.

I am sure most of us have attended a wedding and watched as the bride's father escorted her down the aisle. Once they arrive at the front of the church, the father essentially "gives" his daughter to the handsome young man waiting there. The bride and groom then continue with the wedding ceremony facing the pastor side-by-side, then finish by reciting their vows to one another. The pastor then pronounces them *man and wife*. This gesture of the father giving his daughter away is more than just cultural. God the Father did the same thing! He spent time with Adam preparing him, and then Scripture says, "The Lord God fashioned into a woman the rib which He had taken from the man, *and brought her to the man* [italics added]" (Gen. 2:22). God formed Eve from Adam's side, brought her to Adam, and essentially gave His daughter away, to a prepared and responsible Adam.

Years ago, before I was in ministry, I spent a short time in insurance sales. Part of my sales training was the instruction to concentrate on the woman of the house, appeal to her sense of well-being, and keep making eye contact with her, over and above her husband. This is also true in the automobile sales industry. The idea was that the woman would more readily say yes to certain sales ploys, while the man was more distrustful of salesmen and would be more cautious. Of course, there were many exceptions to this, but by and large, sales training continues to make this assumption. Many salespeople have been successful by undermining the covering, and attempting to appeal to the woman. This was true even from the very beginning, as we have seen with Eve. I personally felt uncomfortable pursuing this tactic, and did not stay in sales very long.

Many of you may have found that the marketplace in general treats women differently than men. When my wife has purchased an item and needs to return it, or has been intimidated on the telephone, she has often asked me to do the follow-up. It is amazing to me to see and hear how differently those who just finished dealing with my wife treat and accommodate me. Usually, I can have a more beneficial outcome for my wife and family by "covering" the situation, and it pleases me that I have been successful in this area. The man's word and presence can make such a difference. I believe that most men want to have this type of impact on behalf of their families, but these days, they often need motivation and encouragement to see themselves in this role. It may seem like a chore, but as part of being an effective coverer, I realize that I am called to "stand in the gap" for those I am covering. '

God was establishing from the beginning that a woman was to be cared for. He established safety for both a man and woman from the beginning. She is to be protected by and be in partnership with a man, under his covering, and that man was to be responsible for the care of his wife. Eldredge wrote, "A man does not go to a woman to get his strength, he goes to offer it" (2001, 115). Ladies if you can just catch a glimpse of this truth: that the almighty, creator God designed relationships in such a way that you are to be cherished and treated with protective, tender, loving care, it would revolutionize how you understand God, your fathers, and your husbands. Unfortunately, the way that men have often treated women has absolutely distorted, and indeed perhaps destroyed, our understanding of the divine design. Men, it is our supreme responsibility to cover our wives and our daughters, and to teach our sons to do the same! *We* will be held accountable accordingly!

Hagar

In Genesis chapter 16, we read of the story of Hagar, who was an Egyptian maidservant to Sarai, Abram's wife. God promised a son to Abram and Sarai, but she was barren. After several years, Sarai offered to Abram an idea to obtain children. She told Abram to treat Hagar as his wife and have children by her. So this great patriarch, who knew God's promise of a son and who was supposed to cover his household with responsible leadership, listened to his anxious and frustrated wife instead of resting under God's covering promise. The result? Domestic turmoil and abuse by Sarai towards Hagar (v. 6). Instead of taking responsibility for the mess, Abram passed the issue on to his wife. Because of her harsh treatment of her maidservant, Hagar fled from their household. Sarai, by suggesting such a sinful alliance out of desperation, stepped out from under her covering. She was very much aware of God's promise of a son for them, but she devised a plan to make sure it occurred. Abram seemed more than willing to "go with the flow" instead of taking leadership based on God's promise for them. This scenario of "helping God out" has been played out countless times in the lives of many, resulting in unwise decisions, conflict, and turmoil.

Hagar was alone and pregnant with nowhere to go. Then verses 8–12 show that God came to Hagar. He found her! He spoke to her, prophesied about her son's future (the blessing), and told her to return to Abram's home. Hagar's response was, "You are a God who sees" (v.

13). This cry is similar to what husbands may hear from their wives: "I wish you would understand me" or "I wish you would see the problem here." God even told Hagar to name her son accordingly (verse 11). The name "Ishmael" in Hebrew means, "God hears." A coverer who sees is one who understands how his wife is feeling, what she is going through, and is one who finds ways to minister to her. While Hagar was definitely not Abram's wife, she was still in his household, under his covering (which was delegated to Sarai). As a result, he was still responsible for how she and his child were to be treated. Abraham's sexual relationship may have been illegitimate, but the child was innocent, and God ultimately cared for him and his mom. Ultimately, God's grace covered Hagar in this case.

Later, in chapter 21 of Genesis, Hagar is sent away again because Sarah (whose name was changed by God by this time) saw contentiousness between Ishmael, Hagar's son, and Isaac, Sarah's son. This time, Abraham (whose name was also changed), provided for Hagar and her son, *and then* sent her away. When her provisions were used up, God appeared to Hagar again, and He continued to provide for her and her son (v. 19–20).

Why is this story important? Remember, God made a *covenant* with Abraham that he would have countless descendants, (Gen. 12:1–3; 17:1–6). The words *cover* and *covenant* come from the same root word in Old English and Latin. The words provide related meanings of promise, being set aside, and being treated with special effort, as in being protected. The Hebrew word *berith*, usually translated as "covenant," would signify *mutual* obligation (Tenney 1978). Even though God made covenant with Abraham for a child of promise, this promise to Abraham "covered" Hagar and her son as well, despite the sinful alliance between her and Abraham, even if it was only in the "many descendants" aspect. Isaac, the eventually child of promise, was born about thirteen years after Ishmael. Genesis 16:10–12 has God speaking to Hagar: "I will greatly multiply your descendants so that they will be too many to count ... And you will bear a son; and you shall call his name Ishmael, because the Lord has given heed to your affliction ...." Today, we know the descendants of Ishmael to be those from the many Arab nations of the world—many descendants, to be sure!

Ruth

The story of Ruth is a wonderful example of proper covering provided to a woman. Ruth was a Moabite. She was married to one of Naomi's sons, who were Hebrews. Naomi's husband dies, then, ten years later, both her sons die, leaving her daughters-in-law also without husbands. One returns home to her people in Moab, but Ruth decides to stay with her mother-in-law. In fact, the Scriptures say that Ruth "clung to her" (Ruth 1:14), and declared, "Your people will be my people, and your God, my God" (Ruth 1:16). Ruth decided to stay under her in-laws' covering and to serve Naomi.

Ruth asks to go and glean in the fields of grain, and with Naomi's permission, she does so. Gleaning was a Hebrew custom of allowing the poor to follow the reapers and servants in order to gather the grain that was left behind. She was attempting, simply and humbly, to provide for herself and Naomi. One of Naomi's relatives, Boaz, owned this particular field. Ruth caught his attention, and when he found out who she was and her intention, he responded with great care and kindness:

> Then Boaz said to Ruth, "Listen carefully, my daughter. Do not go to glean in another field; furthermore, do not go on from this one, but stay here with my maids ... I have commanded the servants *not to touch you* [italics added].

> When you are thirsty go to the water jars and drink from what the servants draw … All that you have done for your mother-in-law after the death of your husband has been fully reported to me, and how you left your father and mother and the land of your birth, and came to a people that you did not previously know. May the Lord reward your work, and your wages be full from the Lord, the God of Israel, *under whose wings you have come to seek refuge*" [italics added]. (Ruth 2:8–12).

Boaz declares *protection* for Ruth, *favor* for Ruth, and *provision* for Ruth. He later invites her to eat at his table, instructs his servants to purposely hold aside additional grain for her to glean, and commands them not to insult her nor mistreat her (v. 14–16). At the end of the story, Boaz marries Ruth, and she becomes the great-grandmother of King David, thus becoming part of the Messianic bloodline. She was not a Jew by birth, but became a Jew by faith, as she accepted God as her God.

There are two primary dynamics working here throughout this story. First, Ruth is very mindful of her role as one who needed a covering, and within that covering, to be a humble blessing to Naomi. This was a win–win for both Naomi and Ruth. Ruth's humility and willingness to serve actually brought her greater provision and honor to Naomi's household. Her respectfulness to her mother-in-law and to Boaz placed her in a place of honor, care, and protection.

On the other hand, Boaz showed great kindness and favor towards Ruth. Because of her attitude and willingness to bless her covering, her mother-in-law Naomi, Boaz took notice. Boaz made sure she was protected, respected, and cared for by those in his employ and in his household. Ruth's approach to her responsibilities made her that much more attractive, and Boaz eventually married her. Boaz went out of his way to love Ruth and provide for her protection and needs. His approach to Ruth, in turn, motivated her to continue to show respect towards him. In fact, the love between Boaz and Ruth even blessed Naomi in her old age, by providing a grandson to her, which restored to her a renewed sense of purpose and life. The impact that can be made by a man and a women expressing love and respect and operating properly under their respective coverings can be immeasurable.

Ultimately, Boaz recognized that Ruth sought to be under the covering of the God of Israel. That desire will cause any man to take notice. A man will notice respect in a woman and a woman will respond to love from a man.

Esther

Esther was an orphan and was raised, or covered, by her cousin Mordecai (Esther 2:7). His wise guidance in Esther's life, as well as her beauty, allowed her to be favored by King Ahasuerus, the king of Persia, who chose her to be his wife and queen.

At the same time, her respectful and compliant manner towards Mordecai (Esther 2:20) carried over to her relationship with her husband, the king. Several times, Esther used the phrase, "If it pleases the king ..." (Esther 5:4, 8 and 7:3).

Even though the king was not a Jew, Esther walked in an attitude of submission and respect. These consistent attitudes won the praise and favor of her husband, King Ahasuerus, and the result was that the king genuinely enjoyed Esther's company and deeply loved her (Esther 5:2–3). This consistent favor eventually placed her in the position of saving her own people, the Jews, from annihilation. Her submission to her husband *empowered* her husband to do the right things!

To honor one's covering will bring honor and blessing back to the one under the covering. The husband will usually respond positively to a wife who respects, honors, and affirms him. Esther was very respectful to her husband, a non-believer in the one true God, who in turn loved Esther all the more. King Ahasuerus not only respected Esther for *her* faith, he overruled a decree that would have destroyed *all* the Jews. Esther's faith had *substance* and motivated the king to honor what was important to his wife!

Mary

Mary was a young virgin, betrothed to Joseph. The angel, Gabriel, told her that she had found favor with God, and was to conceive a son, who would become the Messiah. The angel also stated, "The Holy Spirit will come upon you, and the power of the Most High will *overshadow* [italics added] you; and for that reason the Holy Child shall be called the Son of God" (Luke 2:35). The message here is that the Holy Spirit would *envelop* or *cover* Mary to conceive a divine-natured offspring. The Greek word here, *episkiazo*, is rooted in the word for *overseer* and *coverer* and is from where we derive the word *Episcopal*.

The angel was also making it clear to Mary that God would cover her during this time, as it was a disgrace for an unmarried woman in the Jewish culture to become pregnant. In fact, an angel appeared to Joseph, as well, to inform him that Mary had not violated the customs nor was she unfaithful to him (Matt. 1:18–25). Even when Joseph planned to send Mary away upon learning of her pregnancy, the Scripture says that he did not want to disgrace her, so he planned to send her away secretly (Matt 1:19). A woman found guilty of adultery was to be publicly humiliated and then stoned, but Joseph cared for Mary enough to attempt to prevent that from occurring. Joseph's response was not only because he was described as a righteous man (v. 19), but also because he knew Mary to be a submissive and respectful young woman. And he loved her! Even though Mary knew of the potential turmoil that could occur as a result of her circumstances, her response to the angel sent by God was, "Behold, the bondslave of the Lord; may it be done to me according to your word" (Luke 1:38). Joseph, as well, continued to love Mary and eventually made her his wife.

Finally, even from the cross, Jesus made sure that his mother was cared for. Apparently, Joseph must have died before Jesus began His ministry since he was absent from the gospel narratives. It appears that even Jesus for a time was a son of a single parent! Jesus dispatched John to care for His mother, as if she was his own (John 19:26–27). Essentially, Jesus told John to be Mary's covering.

Submission

There is so much misunderstanding related to this word, and often much abuse in the name of submission. Unfortunately, the church is among the biggest culprits of this misunderstanding. First, submission is *not* a response to control. Because we live in a competitive world, not to mention a fallen world, men and women are often in competition with each other. One result of this belief is to feel threatened by others, especially those in authority. Husbands are often threatened by their wives, and vice versa. The typical response is to try to control what threatens us. Because we see each other as the adversary in things, submission itself is a scary proposition.

Sometimes, there is indeed a threat, where abuse exists, for example. In those cases, the individual must quickly find refuge and a covering that will instead be protective and caring, such as a shelter or a family member. The fact is, men cannot expect submission when they are abusive, when they participate in addictive and irresponsible behaviors, or when they are mean and controlling. A woman must be certain that her husband's strength will be used to protect rather than to harm (Slattery 2001).

The Scriptures give an example of such a situation in 1 Samuel 25. Nabal and his wife, Abigail, were wealthy, having 3,000 sheep and 1,000 goats. While David was traveling with his men through the wilderness, he heard that Nabal was shearing his sheep nearby. David sent ten men to request respectfully of Nabal some assistance in the way of provision and food. Nabal was described as a man who was "harsh and evil in his dealings ..." (v. 3), and true to this description, he not only refused, but insulted the soldiers and David. King David was so angry, he planned to overrun and destroy Nabal and his household. Abigail was mortified and went out to meet David with gifts; she graciously and submissively apologized for her husband's behavior, and in doing so, saved her home and family. David responded very kindly to her and blessed her. Later, when Abigail returned home, she found her husband was partying and was drunk.

The next day she told her husband how she felt and what she did to be kind to David; Nabal's heart became "as a stone" (v. 37). About ten days later, the Lord struck Nabal dead. Abigail's humility evidently won David's heart, as she later became his wife. It may appear that Abigail became unsubmissive to Nabal, but she acted to save her household and home. She did not excuse Nabal's behavior, nor act as an enabler. Rather, she acted the best way she could in protecting the dignity of her household, which is often necessary when dealing with an evil, abusive, and unworthy covering.

Second, submission is *not* mindless, strict obedience. The Greek word for submission is *hupotasso* and is a military term which means to "put oneself under" or "recognize and follow the authority" of another. This describes the posture of the *willingness* to be "covered" by the recognized authority, not some kind of blind obedience. An individual can demand obedience, but not submission! A person can obey because he or she has to, but submission is willingness, a choice, a decision, to take on the posture of a subordinate.

When a woman chooses to marry a man, she is essentially choosing to come under his covering. Scriptures do not tell a wife to "obey" her husband, but to submit. *Children* are to *obey* their parents (Eph. 6:1; Col. 3:20). They are to do so because their covering parents are their authority and protectors. However, children are not required to obey parents who may lead them into lawlessness or sexual abuse, for example. One passage that seems to suggest obedience for a wife is 1 Peter 3:5–6:

> For in this way in former times the holy women also, who hoped in God, used to adorn themselves, being submissive to their own husbands; just as Sarah obeyed Abraham, calling him lord, and you have become her children if you do what is right without being frightened by any fear.

The word translated "obeyed" is really a form of *hupotasso*, which indicates that Sarah's obedience was a willing submissive posture. A wife is to honor and respect her husband, to come willingly under his authority, which is designed by God to be her covering. Submission is for husbands, too, as men are to come under God's authority and covering. This is true in the marketplace, as well. When we agree to a job offer, part of what we are agreeing to is to submit to our new boss and supervisors.

This concept operates within the church as well. When we find a church that we like, we are called to submit to the leadership, in particular, the pastor of that church and its elders. This is a proposition based on the willingness of the church member to follow the leadership. Our responsibility is to be a willing servant of the God-ordained leader, as well as each other, and to support the vision of that church. When people leave a church, they are making the statement that they are no longer willing to submit to the pastor, regardless of what other reasons may be expressed.

On the other hand, a good and wise church leader is willing to develop others who will one day provide oversight and leadership. They are interested in seeing others reach their callings and dreams, rather than be threatened by their giftedness. A good future "coverer" will only be as good as his willingness to submit to those in authority over him. The story of Elisha and Elijah is an excellent example. Elisha served Elijah faithfully *before* he was able to move with power and authority in his own ministry (2 Kings 2).

Scripture also speaks of another aspect of submission, namely, the *mutual* submission of all believers to Christ and one another. We are instructed to work together in harmony, even within the roles that have been designed by God. The roles are for function, not for lording over someone. This command is found in Ephesians 5:21, before we read about wives submitting to their husbands and husbands loving their wives. In addition, the heart of the matter is expressed in Philippians 2:3–4: "Do nothing from selfishness or empty conceit, but with humility of mind regard one another *as more important than yourselves*; [italics added] do not merely look out for your own personal interests, but also for the interest of others." Also, James 3:14–16 provides a powerful warning against selfishness and arrogance:

> But if you have bitter jealousy and selfish ambition in your heart, do not be arrogant and so lie against the truth. This wisdom is not that which comes down from above, but is

earthly, natural, demonic. For where jealousy and selfish ambition exist, there is disorder and every evil thing.

The apostle Paul, as inspired by the Holy Spirit, is raising the stakes. In Ephesians 5:22–33, a careful reader will understand that submission by the wife is a *response* to the sacrificial love of her husband. This is to be a win–win relationship. Husbands, if you want to experience a wife that truly desires to follow your lead, then love her as Christ loved the church: Jesus gave Himself up for her! Being willing to *sacrifice* or delay our own agendas, indeed even our lives, for our wives' benefit, is our calling. Sacrifice is complete selflessness. Wives, if you desire to see your husband cover you and provide love and leadership in the family, then *respectfully* submit to his role over you. One is not to operate in the absence of the other! When the husband is demanding submission from his wife, he is in reality demanding blind obedience, which is not God's design. Submission is given, not taken. It is the *willing* acceptance of another's authority.

Very early in our marriage, my wife and I were often in conflict, and it was usually about my desire to "feel like" the leader of the home by having my way. One particular morning, about two years after our wedding day, my wife and I were having an argument that left us both upset and in tears. I went to take a shower, still upset, and I had an open vision in the shower! I saw a cloud of dust that engulfed me and someone else with whom I was fighting and wrestling. It was not clear to me at that moment who the other figure was. After a few moments, the fighting stopped, the cloud slowly receded, and I noticed myself, flat on my back on the ground, beaten in battle, while the victorious figure standing over me became clear—I recognized Him to be Jesus!

The message was very clear to me that day. I was not just fighting with my wife; I was fighting the Lord Himself! I was so bent on my way that I did not understand that I needed to submit to God's way, first and foremost. I was hurting my standing before my wife because I was actually demanding my way rather than God's way. I had to learn submission too, in order to lead. Just as in the military: a good and effective leader is first a good subordinate! Before I could become a good "coverer," I had to come under my covering.

Finally, submission does not mean that women are to be considered less valuable than men are. The roles and temperaments may be different, but men and women are to treat each other as equal and valuable in each other's eyes. One of the misnomers of feminism is in the relationship between men and women, namely, that equality means *sameness.* The argument is that our society oppresses women and that they need to be seen as and treated as men. Unisex fashion is one of many results of this thinking. The feminist agenda has been used by Satan to tear down our society, and womanhood, as created by God, has been maligned and subverted (Zampino 2004). All that is truly feminine—the loveliness of her body, the sacredness of the fruit of her womb, her ability to nurture, her intuitiveness and relational skills--has been denigrated, sneered at, and belittled (Zampino 2004).

If women feel loved for who they are and for their uniqueness, then it is easier for them to come under such a covering. Remember, a loving covering also protects the dignity of those under such a covering. When a woman feels loved, dignified and honored, she functions with respect towards her husband and with power and influence. In turn, a husband often responds lovingly to his wife's attempts to find the hero in him (Slattery 2001). The beautiful reciprocal nature of a loving marriage is God's design.

Feminists have preached that a woman's independence is tied

Created for Covering

directly to her sexuality, which is exploited by men. Even within feminism, there is confusion as to how this plays out. Bardon (1978) suggests that there are at least three segments of feminists thinking. One segment teaches increased heterosexual activity and freedom for women, and it places emphasis on a woman's inherent right to sexual pleasure. Another group of vehement feminists is furious at this position and in general feels that a withdrawal from sexual activity is needed because any type of heterosexual contact is exploitative of females. A third core of women's liberationists is so angry and vindictive toward males that they espouse a general movement toward female homosexuality (Bardon 1978).

The feminists, however, are generally and conspicuously silent when it comes to the devastation of pornography and the *exploitation* of women that is inherently a part of the pornography industry. Pornography is not a love for the women being viewed, but rather a hatred of women who are seen as nothing more than objects of personal pleasure.

Also, Professor Sidney Callahan has said, "We will never climb to equality over the dead bodies of own children" (Mathewes-Green 1994). The damage done to women during "legal" abortions is very rarely discussed, as well. In my experience alone, of all the women that have come to counseling for either depression or anxiety, 60 percent of them have had at least one abortion earlier in their life. Other studies have shown similar correlations.

Is it really necessary to even proclaim that men and women *are* different? The truth is, nothing can change the fact that men and women are different. Our anatomy is different. Our body design is different. The wiring of our brains is different. Our emotions and the related approach to life are different. The differences are to complement one another in marriage so that oneness can occur. It is true by God's design. In God's design, different does not mean less valuable. Exploitation of either gender is evil and leads to a great distortion of God's design. Men and women are indeed equal in worth, but are different physiologically and in function. Both men and women are heirs to the kingdom of God. Galatians 3:28–29 says, "There is neither Jew nor Greek, there is neither slave nor free man, there is neither male nor female; for you are one in Christ Jesus. And if you belong to Christ, then you are Abraham's descendants, heirs according to promise." This passage does not promote a unisex society. Rather, it is simply stating that we all have the same standing through the finished work of Christ.

Submission, therefore, is not a dirty word. We all find that we can gladly submit to someone we trust and to whom we know has our best interest in mind. Gentlemen, that is truly the case with regards to our Abba Father. Can we say with confidence that our wives, children and anyone who we oversee, are just as assured in us?

CHAPTER 5
Covering versus Controlling

Over the years, I have had several men come to me saying what amounts to this: "My wife has been asking me to lead the family and take care of things. But often when I do, I am told that I am too controlling! What's the deal?" These guys were in what is called, in counseling, a double bind, or in the vernacular, burned if they did and burned if they didn't. One of the greatest paradoxes in marriage is a wife's desire to have her husband lead her and her unwillingness to follow him when he does (Slatttery, 2001). Over the last forty to fifty years, our society has been subtly and insidiously dealt a bill of goods that today has placed men and women in such gender confusion that the roles we play are all over the charts. Feminism, homosexuality, abuse, and fatherlessness in particular have rendered the male gender weak and confused. One the other hand, the message has become, "I can be independent," "live a life with no restraints," and "I can have it all."

I have counseled many young people, college-aged through mid-twenties men and women, who have expressed gender confusion in their sexuality and in their role relationships, which is troubling. I have found that women and especially men have not been properly equipped to deal with the stresses of life, mainly because of (1) abuses or (2) they have not experienced a proper covering, model, and influence in their early life. Our society has become so self-centered or self-oriented, (this includes many parents), that we are no longer considerate of others and we no longer know how to be subordinate and respectful to others. The essence of this crisis is the debate of who is in control.

Being under a covering is not the same as being controlled. In like manner, being a coverer is not a sanction to be controlling. There is a subtle, yet important difference. The Webster's dictionary definition of *control* when used as a verb is to "exercise authority over, as to regulate." The word *control* in the noun form is "dominion," "mastery," "rule," or "governance." Other synonyms are to *impose*, which means to force upon another or to take unfair advantage over another, or to *dictate*, which means to prescribe or demand with authority.

It is very clear in Scripture that Adam *and* Eve were to take dominion or control over creation *together*, not take dominion over each other (Gen. 1:27–28)! We are also taught to take mastery over sin in our lives (Rom. 6:12, 14). In contrast, as shown in an earlier chapter, to cover is to be over someone or something, as in to protect, to defend, to guide, or to provide purpose. Life to a controller is about him, while to a coverer, it is all about those for whom he is responsible. Controllers are self-centered and bring harm and hurt. Coverers provide safety, security, and direction.

Characteristics

In the book, *Avoiding Mr. Wrong (And What To Do If You Didn't)*, by Stephen Arterburn and Meg Rinck (2000), there is an excellent list of the characteristics of a controller. A controlling person (man or woman):

- Is critical, negative, and mean most of the time
- Is easily irritated over small things
- Tends to be stubborn and unteachable
- Says "it's my way or the highway"
- Does not deviate—likes established ways of doing things
- Will tell you always when he disagrees with you or does not like something that you are doing
- Uses "black or white" or "all or nothing" thinking
- Is closed minded; other options are not considered
- Is imperative, demanding and intense
- Chooses "doing things right" over relationships
- Is very disciplined, to a fault
- Sets very high standards for self *and* others
- Seems driven in everything he does
- Gets irritated and angry when others mess up
- Takes other people's failures as personal insults
- Is uncomfortable with emotions—his and yours
- Holds the need to dominate, be in control, have the last word, as more important than relationships
- Is resentful and often bitter
- Is probably much more insecure than he appears
- Values people based on only how similar they are to him
- Attracts a strange group of compliant people in his relationships
- Does not do the work, but *tells you* how and when and what ought to be done
- Looks down on women and girls (if a woman, she may hate men)

Often, in reality, a controlling person is very insecure. They are driven, in fact, by fear. Their fear of being ridiculed, rejected, and hurt drives them to be sure they are the aggressor, which serves as a defense mechanism. They are often cowards when pushed. Such a person will not create a safe environment.

When parents plant seeds of rejection or failure in their children, these young people may grow up to be controllers. The lie they believe is that no matter what they do, they can never measure up or be acceptable. The result can be a response where the individual attempts to feel in control over something and will try to control others as a way to prevent further hurt and pain.

The victims of a controller believe they are without power. However, the truth is if an individual were to challenge a controller, the controller would often back down. The lie is that a controller is in control, when in truth he is *out of control,* lives under false beliefs, and needs counseling and a healing and settling touch from God!

In contrast, a coverer is one who allows for and welcomes participation from those he oversees. To accept other perspectives and wisdom is to the benefit of all involved. It behooves the husband to hear from his wife, especially with respect to major decisions and in the areas delegated to her by her husband. Neither the husband nor the wife is called to do it all, and delegation is very appropriate. Even in the corporate world, business partners have specific areas that they are responsible for, all for the purpose of running the business smoothly. Delegation is still working together, but it simply allows for the practical application for focused leadership. For example, in most cases, I have found that the wife is better at managing the details of the home, the kids, and important dates. It is a mistake for the husband to not honor that and appreciate how well his wife can hold things together at home. I know that I am very thankful for my wife and her attentiveness to things that are harder for me.

Essentially, the woman is *empowered* to make decisions when her husband delegates areas of responsibility to her. When God delegated to Adam the oversight of the earth, Adam was empowered to go forth. When God delegates to men our responsibilities, we likewise, are empowered to function accordingly. When husbands delegate to their wives, the understanding is that we can trust them and depend upon them to do what is necessary for the well-being of the family. To be clear, delegation alludes to function and gifting, but the marriage couple is to work together as one. When parents delegate to children, the children are learning the importance of contributing to the "vision," of the family, and they will eventually see the importance of working together, even if they are complaining now.

Also, a coverer has the courage to know his limitations and is indeed willing to see others excel in areas in which he may be weak, all for the benefit of the common good. He may remain responsible for the ultimate outcome, but utilizing *and* appreciating those that serve with and under him brings about positive outcomes. This is what mentoring and coaching are all about. For example, I was asked by our senior pastor to provide leadership and a covering for our church's worship team, but as a musician, even I know my musical limitations. As a result, I have relied on singers and musicians who are more gifted than I am to help with the "nuts and bolts," if you will, of making a song sound good. Together, with mutual submission, we saw a spirit of worship, with God being the One honored.

Also, a coverer sees mistakes as growth areas, rather than reasons to be irritated, critical, or to fly off the handle at someone. Sometimes, a coverer needs additional time in training or mentoring. A responsible coverer will see mistakes and failures for what they often are—mistakes and failures—not personal vendettas or a statements of rejection toward others. Even after a failure, a good coverer will re-release the one who failed with forgiveness and renewed empowerment. After all, isn't this exactly how God, our Father, treats us? We all would be in trouble if God were like many parents and supervisors. Nor is our Father as the idols and gods of the world, who have to be appeased through many rituals and even human sacrifices, just to prevent those gods from lambasting the one who fell short. Instead, our Father sees us through the finished work of His Son, Jesus, and sins and mistakes are covered by His blood and love.

As we have seen from the beginning, the Lord God is more interested in teaching us His ways, *then* setting us free to function according to our calling. God desires to empower us to do His will. While it is true that God is in control, He does not control us nor force us to make choices. The negative things that we may encounter when we choose to come out from under covering are *consequences of OUR behavior*. God is not responsible for our choices. He has provided direction, guidance, commandments, and love. We live either the good consequences to God's ways, or the bad consequences to our rebellion and selfishness.

Controllers are motivated by insecurity and fear of rejection. Perhaps, during much of their lives, they lived in environments where things were so out of control that now they have to be in control of at least *something*. The thought is, the more I appear to be in control, the more I am, in fact, in control. The drive for control is often a defense mechanism to protect the controller from rejection. The opposite is usually the case. There may be an appearance of control, but in reality, the damaged relationships that occur become evidence of chaos, loss of relationships, and loss of control. "When men and women refuse to work *together*, it can be a subtle form of warfare which can lead to chaos" (Vanier 2003). Power over others will never diminish fears. It will only increase them.

Types of Controllers

According to Arterburn and Rinck (2000), there are several types of controllers. The first is the "robot." This controller is the strong, silent type, is afraid of emotions (his and others), and believes emotions actually threaten his sense of control. This individual has difficulty with communication and usually lives in avoidance and denial. This type of controller usually has experienced traumatic experiences, a sudden loss or pain over time, and they cram their emotions deep down inside. They may see this as biblical "self-control," but the truth is they are simply denying the fact that all humans have emotions. They often claim to have no feelings at all, even in the light of disturbing issues. Emotions can be held down only for so long, and they will eventually emerge through illness, temper, or other damaging means. Feelings are never buried dead, they are buried alive (Arterburn & Rinck 2000).

Early in our marriage, I would say to my wife, "You can't possibly feel that way ..." Well, she did "feel that way," and I ignored the fact that feelings should not be ignored, neither by my wife nor by me. By my comments, I was invalidating her identity and her potential insight into a situation. Understandably, my wife did not embrace my ignorance and my approach to her. At those times, her *feelings* towards *me* were, well, something I could not ignore!

We really cannot tell someone how to feel, nor can we deny that we have any feelings. We do well to explore *why* they may feel the way they do, then to respond with affirmation then with appropriate and responsible behavior. Such response develops safety in relationships. If we do try to validate feelings, that does not mean we are attempting to live by our feelings. To let our feelings control us or to ignore them are opposite ends of a spectrum, and neither is healthy.

Another common type of controller is a violent controller (Arterburn & Rinck 2000). These individuals do not take responsibility for their behaviors. They claim that others *make* them act the way they do and even expect the other party to do all the apologizing for *causing* them to lose their temper. Simply stated, their behavior is not *their* fault. Anger and intimidation are the typical modes of operation for this type of controller. Individuals who live in such an environment feel unsafe. The unpredictability of this person also causes others to be controlled to the point where they will avoid all forms of irritation, just to prevent the controller from exploding. Even if these controllers have not struck their spouses, the constant throwing of objects, slamming doors, etc., will cause their spouses to wonder when they indeed may be physically harmed. This binds the victims and forces them to walk on eggs at all times.

Verbal abusers are violent controllers also. They verbally intimidate and ridicule those they try to control. Verbal controllers also blame others for "making them mad." Often, emotional wounds that result are more difficult to heal. These controllers can cause pain that can haunt others for many years. The little ditty that we as children used to recite, "Sticks and stones can broke my bones but words can never hurt me," *is a lie*. Words do hurt. Proverbs 15:4 says, "A soothing tongue is a tree of life, but perversion in it crushes the spirit."

Finally, there are male-chauvinist controllers (Arterburn & Rinck 2000). These are men who believe that women are actually inferior to men. They tend to be very possessive of their wives and families. In fact, they see their families as simply possessions. They also are very jealous and do things like screen calls, check texts messages, eavesdrop, check their wives' pocketbooks, etc.

If you are sincerely interested in changing from a controller to a coverer, then several things will be necessary. First, develop a healing and intimate relationship with Christ so that He can heal your insecurity, hurts, and fear of rejection. Remember, God will never leave you nor forsake you, He loves you, and He desires to equip you to be your best and to build healthy relationships. Seek out

His presence, for He is safe; seek out His love, for He is accepting; seek out His ways, for He is a wonderful Coverer! Next, let go of perfectionistic behaviors, drop the performance orientation, and become less demanding of self and others. Freedom of performance can be one of the most liberating states of being in which to live. Remember, we are human beings, not human doings!

In closing, you may need to consult with a pastor or a counselor in order to determine the pain in your own life that may need a healing touch from God. Therapy, inner healing, or deliverance and trusted support can be aids to you. Next, remember that the problem is primarily about *you*, not others. Jesus taught, "Why do you look at the speck in your brother's eye, but do not notice the log that is in your own eye … You hypocrite, first take the log out of your own eye, and then you will see clearly to take out the speck that is in your brother's eye" (Luke 6:41–42). The essential posture is that of surrender and humility. Someone can be a good leader only when they learn to be a good subordinate. Surrender in the Kingdom of God is not powerlessness – it actually brings empowerment!

CHAPTER 6

When the Covering Is Lost

Adam and Eve were living happily ever after. They were partners in dominion over God's creation on earth. There was peace in their relationship and in the land. Then they ate of the fruit of the forbidden tree. And everything changed. God's design took a beating because of the irresponsibility of Adam, a self-glorifying agenda, and both Adam and Eve's disobedience. Just as creation was effected by Lucifer's iniquity and rebellion, the earth was once again thrust into turmoil. Again, God spoke and acted with redemption in mind. He *covered* Adam and Eve's nakedness and shame. He then prophesied to Eve that her seed, the coming Messiah, would crush the head of the seed of the serpent, even though the serpent's seed would bruise His heel (Gen. 3:15).

Then God proclaimed a curse to the serpent, to the man, and to the woman. Within the *context of this curse*, God declared to Adam and Eve what they now could expect to be true in their lives together, because of their disobedience and sin. Genesis 3:16 says, "To the woman He said, 'I will greatly multiply your pain in childbirth, in pain you will bring forth children; Yet your desire will be for your husband, and he will rule over you'." This statement has been misunderstood for years, but with careful reading, it truly provides an understanding of what takes place between husbands and wives as a result of the beginning of sin in the Garden of Eden.

We have heard that even though the woman was to experience pain in childbirth, her desire, sexually, for her husband would remain intact. Upon further review, if you will, this Hebrew word, *teshuwqah,* translated as *desire,* is found only two other places in Scripture: in Genesis 4:7 and Song of Solomon 7:10. In Genesis 4:7, God is speaking to Cain just before he kills his brother Abel: "If you do well, will not your countenance be lifted up? And if you do not do well, sin is crouching at the door; and its *desire* [emphasis added] is for you, but you must master it." This word has a negative connotation. God is saying that Eve would desire to dominate and overwhelm her husband, just as sin wanted to overcome Cain! The word can be better understood as not just to "*turn* to" but with the intent to "*turn* against." Women would strive to control, manipulate, rule, and run their husbands' decisions and desires (Littleton 1988). This would be a result of Adam's sin, and God is simply informing humankind that conflict and fight for control is now a part of relationships.

Man's response to this? "And he will rule over you." This is not the same word in Hebrew that is found earlier in Genesis 1:28, when God told the couple to "rule" over the earth in a responsible, benign kind of rule. No, this "rule" is the kingly, crush-him-down-and-become-an-imperial-master sort of rule (Littleton 1988). Man would respond by trying to take back the control that he perceives his wife is trying to wrestle from him. The "battle of the sexes" did not begin with the Bobby Riggs vs. Billie Jean King historic tennis match that took place in September of 1973. It began right here, all because Adam chose to come out from under God's covering.

There are many ways that a man can lose his effectiveness as a covering over his wife and family, which in turn will render him ineffective in other arenas. The first and most important way is to deliberately go against what he knows to be right and choose to come out from under his God-covering. There are many examples in Scripture, but I will briefly mention three.

The first is Eli, the priest in Israel, just before God calls a king to rule the people. The story is found in 1 Samuel, chapters 1 through 4. Eli had two sons who were also priests, but they were described as "worthless men" who did not know the Lord (1 Sam. 2:12). As you read the story, it becomes clear that Eli was a weak leader, knowing what was right, but not doing it. Instead of sacrificing the best part of the offering to God, his sons, Phinehas and Hophni, would keep it for themselves (1 Sam. 2:12, 29). They were also immoral and would have sex with women who served near the temple (1 Sam. 2:22). God said that Eli would not rebuke his sons (1 Sam. 3:13). Eli weakly attempted to correct them, but they would not listen to his voice (1 Sam. 2:25). The inference is that Eli wilted in his attempts to correct his sons. God sent a messenger to Eli and told him that God would hold him accountable for his son's actions. Why? Read verse 29 of First Samuel chapter 2: "Why do you kick at My sacrifice and My offering which I have commanded in My dwelling, and *honor your sons above Me*, by making *yourselves* [emphasis added] fat with the choicest of every offering of My people Israel?" God told Eli that his own example encouraged his sons, since he also participated in the short-changing of the sacrifices and was robbing God.

God said Eli's household would lose its influence (v. 30, 31, 33), that He would raise up another priest from outside his family (v. 35) and that his sons would be killed (v. 34). Later, Eli died due to an accident, and he was described as "old and heavy" (1 Sam. 4:18). Other parts of his household were left in turmoil as well. His daughter-in-law, Phinehas' wife, died giving birth and their son was named Ichabod, which means, "the glory of the Lord departed from Israel" (1 Sam. 4:19–21). God did hold Eli's sons directly *responsible* for their actions, but he held Eli *accountable* for his example to them and lack of discipline in his home. Eli was their covering, their father, and because of his weak leadership in the home, rebellion, immorality, destruction, and weakened influence occurred.

The next example is Samuel, the priest who followed Eli, interestingly enough. Samuel was mentored by Eli (of all people), and performed many righteous deeds as judge and prophet to the people. However, he appointed his two sons, Joel and Abijah, as judges over Israel (1 Sam. 8:1). They did not walk after their father's ways; they sought out dishonest gains, accepted bribes and perverted justice (1 Sam. 8:3). What happened? The elders of Israel all *came to Samuel*, not the sons, to complain (1 Sam. 8:4–5). Their behavior came back on the dad, Samuel. Samuel, however, did petition to the Lord, his covering, as to what to do, and he did as God instructed.

Finally, the example of Moses may surprise some. In Exodus chapter four, after a long dialog with God, Moses was commissioned by God to return to Egypt to be the deliverer of the Israelites. Moses gathers his family, his wife, Zapporah, and his sons, and returns to Egypt. Three seemingly obscure verses appear in this story:

> Now it came about at the lodging place on the way that the Lord met him and sought to put him to death. Then Zapporah took a flint and cut off her son's foreskin and threw it at Moses' feet, and she said, "You are indeed a bridegroom of blood to me." So He let him alone ... (Exod. 4:24–26).

Moses, knowing his true heritage as a Hebrew, evidently did not circumcise his boys. Zapporah, who was not a Hebrew, performed the circumcision instead, and by doing so, saved Moses' life! As coverer over his home, God held Moses accountable, even to the point of death, for not performing this rite, which was to symbolize the separation of God's people from the rest of the world. As a Hebrew, Moses knew very well what was required, but here he stepped out from under God's covering. It was not the wife's duty to perform this rite, but rather the father's. Moses had to have his own house in order, in order to be the effective deliverer of the Hebrews he was to be.

Gentlemen, our wives and children are watching us and looking to us. Are we walking under the covering of our Father, or are we doing our own thing? If I were to say, "Like father, like son," would you be squirming, or would you feel proud? Family patterns, or curses, can be broken under the blood of Christ—that's the good news of the Gospel! You see, being a good or bad covering is first and foremost a spiritual dynamic. That is why it so vitally important how our lives are portrayed to those under our care and influence. If you happen to be a man who has left his family, you have placed them in a vulnerable and unsafe place, and God will hold you accountable. We cannot run and hide from our responsibilities despite our best efforts to do so.

Remember, if the devil is successful in taking out the leaders, he knows the effects trickle down to those who have lost the covering. A break in the covering or the spiritual hedge placed around families is what the devil is looking for in order to have access to others. In military warfare, if the field commander is "taken out," often the rest of the soldiers experience confusion and are vulnerable to be quickly defeated. The same is true in spiritual warfare. Once a breach occurs, Satan knows he can be more effective in producing turmoil and destruction in the lives of individuals. I have seen this happen over and over again in many individuals and families.

Wives and daughters do not despise the covering that your husband or father provides. If he is under God's covering, then you are truly blessed. If he is not, encourage him to be the man you love him to be, letting him know you are counting on him and that you believe in him.

Many other influences cause a covering to weaken or disappear. Let's look at several.

Drunkenness

When husbands and fathers bring drugs, alcohol, and strong drink into their homes and lives, the devil has been invited to have access into the home as well. There is no good thing that occurs with alcohol or drug addiction in the life of the coverer. He may even be drinking outside the home, but he is still, nevertheless affecting his household. It is estimated that 9.8 million men are problem drinkers and about 6.6 million children less than eighteen years of age live in households with at least one alcoholic parent (Alcoholic-Information. com, 2012). In fact, "Addiction is now the *number one* public health issue in the United States" (AACC 2009, 1).

Some direct effects of households influenced by alcohol include the estimate that 40 percent of all traffic fatalities are related to the abuse of alcohol (National Institute of Health 2002, 1). In addition, alcohol contributes to 100,000 deaths a year, making it the *third* leading cause of preventable death in this country (Alcohol-Information. com, 2012). Finally, two-thirds of victims who suffered violence by an intimate (a current or former spouse, boyfriend, or girlfriend) reported that alcohol had been a factor (About.com: Alcoholism 2003, 1). So, drunkenness and the effects of coverers who participate in this evil and destructive behavior cause abuse, death, and many other types of sorrow and pain. Very unsafe indeed!

God commanded that Moses, as well as his sons, refrain from drinking strong drink when they came into God's presence, and this was to be a "perpetual statute throughout your generations" (Lev. 10:9). God called such a behavior "profane" and "unclean." While this was directly related to those who were to operate in the priestly function, all husbands are coverers and considered the priests of their home, and they are not to be out from under God's covering. I do not believe it is by accident that strong drink is often called "spirits." Those who misuse alcohol and drugs lose their faculties and open their spirits up to thoughts and behaviors that are detrimental, demonic, and evil. Financial problems, abuse, or neglect often accompanies drunkenness and substance abuse in the home. Proverbs 23:29–35 says:

> Who has woe? Who has sorrow? Who has contentions? Who has complaining? Who has wounds without cause? Who has redness of eyes? Those who linger long over wine. Do not look on the wine when it is red, when it sparkles in the cup, when it goes down smoothly; At the last it bites like a serpent and stings like a viper. Your eyes will see strange things and your mind will utter perverse things. And you will be like the one who lies down in the middle of the sea, or like one who lies down on the top of a mast. They struck me, but I did not become ill; They beat me, but I did not know it. When shall I awake? I will seek another drink.

The last few phrases are consistent with the old adage that when someone is drunk, they "feel no pain." I used to hear my father utter those words often as he became an alcoholic in his later years. He also became very contentious, especially when drunk, picking quarrels with anyone he was with. He would say vulgar and "perverse things," as well, when he was drunk, which is common when strong drink takes over, making people lose their faculties. Sadly, at the end of his life, despite efforts by many to reach out to him, he died alone with few friends and an alienated family.

Since that time, I have to say, I have come to appreciate my father. He was a good man and a good father. He struggled with the hurts that life tends to bring to us all. As a World War II combat veteran; as someone who lived through the Great Depression in the 1920s; as a man whose father died of cirrhosis of the liver, directly due to alcohol addiction; as a husband who lost his wife (my mother) to cancer early in their lives together; I understand his desire to "medicate" the pain. When I think of my dad now, I can recall the good things he imparted to me. Things such as a strong work ethic, loyalty, dedication, commitment, faithfulness, service to country and family, the importance of faith in God, and being a coach to many youngsters who were rejected, are some of the many aspects that he modeled for me as my covering. For that, I am eternally grateful.

My father was a third generation alcoholic. Children of alcoholics are four times more likely to become alcoholics than are children from non-alcoholic homes (Sarason & Sarason 1999). This behavior can have an element of "modeling," that can be a curse and/or spirit that is carried from one generation to another. Since I accepted Jesus Christ as an eighteen year old, it is by His grace and the life changing power of the Holy Spirit that I can say that I do not fear ever becoming an alcoholic. I am convinced that this pattern has been broken, and I can be confident that my children do not have to contend with this spirit—as long as they remain under a similar covering. That means that my sons are to remain under the direct covering of the Lord God and my daughters under a covering of a Godly, temperate husband.

Sexual Sins

It is incredible to think how something so beautiful and pleasurable that was designed by God to be enjoyed within the marriage bond, has been so distorted by Satan to bring so much abuse, disease, pain, and perversion into our world. This is such a strong spirit of deception that we really need to be vigilant to stay under God's covering in this area. For example, there is a worldwide repulsive phenomenon of trafficking women and girls as sex slaves, as reported by Malarek (2003). The trafficking of women is now the third largest illicit moneymaker in the world, after illegal weapons and drugs (Malarek 2003). Corrupt officials in many countries perpetuate this "industry." These men are hideously abusing their covering responsibilities, to say the least. Since no covering exists, these women and girls have been exposed to rape, abuse, torture, HIV/AIDS, STDs, poor nutrition, and drug and alcohol addiction (Malarek 2003).

Pornography is a *powerful* force that weakens and destroys a covering. In fact, I believe it is a spiritual, demonic force. Research done by a ministry that directly deals with sexual sins has found that about 70 percent of women in pornography are survivors of childhood sexual abuse (Mastering Life 2006). About 60 percent of all websites are sexual in nature (Mastering Life 2006). The estimated annual pornography revenue worldwide is $57 *billion*, with $13 billion coming from the United States alone (Mastering Life 2006). The average age of someone seeking help for pornography addiction is thirty to thirty-five years old (Mastering Life 2006). Think about that. That's a realistic age for a man to be in the role of a coverer. If that man has such an addiction, it will and is affecting his relationships and those in his family, and often in his workplace.

Findings have shown that one in seven calls to Focus on The Family's Pastoral Care hotline is about Internet pornography

(Mastering Life 2006). Also, 47 percent of Christians admit that pornography is a major problem *in their homes* (Mastering Life 2006). How desensitized have we become? Well, one in five born-again Christians believes that viewing magazines with nudity and sexually explicit pictures is morally acceptable and 36 percent of Christians say co-habitation is morally acceptable (Mastering Life 2006). Brothers and sisters, what are we thinking? Has the body of Christ been that deceived?

I know of a family in which the husband and wife would often watch pornographic videos together because they wanted to have, as they put it, a little more spice in their sex life. *After* bringing this force into the home, the husband struggled with employment issues, they had financial struggles, their two teenage daughters were both diagnosed with bi-polar disorders, were placed on heavy medication, and slept around with their boyfriends. The father could not understand why his life and household was so chaotic. Of course, other circumstances contributed to such chaos, but this was the beginning.

Pornography is not a "private vice" where no one gets hurt. It is by no means a safe venture. The wife especially is hurt and humiliated when she knows that her husband is looking upon other women for his pleasures. This can be considered an "affair of the heart." Once this evil is invited and accepted into the home, the covering will inevitably and quickly break down and affect other individuals who are in the household.

Sexual abuse and incest are also abhorrent behaviors, which destroy the concept of covering. Obviously, those who are under such a covering no longer can see themselves as protected or cherished. They need to remove themselves from such a household and find a new covering that can provide protection, care, and healing. Studies have shown that one out of five boys and one out of three girls are victims of sexual abuse before they reach the age of eighteen (Survivors of Incest Anonymous 2007). Abuse also results in various social maladjustments such as alcoholism, drug addiction, self-injury, prostitution, promiscuity, eating disorders, migraines, sleeping disorders and phobias (Survivors of Incest Anonymous 2007).

An abusive covering can inflict wounds and pain in children for many years to come. Often, the chaos that develops in such households is transferred to the households of their victims as they try to maneuver through adulthood and their own marriages later in life. God makes it clear in Scripture that incest and sex with any family member is strictly forbidden (Lev. 18:6-17; 1 Cor. 5:1–5).

Adultery is also a covering buster, often for two households. If a husband has an affair with a married woman, for example, not only is he coming out from under his covering, God Himself, but he is also leading the other woman out from under her covering. In both situations, this undermining produces repercussions within both families. I believe that God holds the *man* primarily responsible for the fallout that occurs in *both* of these households. When King David engaged in an affair with Bathsheba, God sent the prophet Nathan *to David* and dealt with him directly (2 Sam. 12:1–15). David's response? "I have sinned *against the Lord* [italics added] (2 Sam. 12:13). Even though David violated Bathsheba and murdered her husband, Uriah, he knew, ultimately, against whom he had sinned.

Unfaithfulness in any form destroys trust. That is indeed true when adultery occurs and typically, trust takes time to be regained. Adultery can also bring disease, as sexually transmitted diseases (STDs) can be a very real danger. Again, this can affect more than one household and many lives. We need to be mindful of Jesus' teaching here. Matthew 5:28 says, "But I say to you that everyone who looks at a woman with lust for her has already committed adultery with her in his heart." A husband has *no* business being on "chat rooms" with other women, nor *pursuing* other women outside of his marriage. This will weaken his ability to cover, to say the least, and make he and his family vulnerable to attacks from the devil.

A couple came to counseling because the wife learned that her husband had a short, two-month affair with a co-worker. After a couple of sessions, I learned that the husband was into pornography and demanded that his wife participate in sadomasochist (S & M) lovemaking. The fantasy pursuits of his gathered steam, and he began to look elsewhere for his fulfillment. The pain from the affair, but not these sexual practices, was devastating to the wife. While they were church-going people, they stopped coming to counseling after just a few weeks because neither wanted to deal with the "moral" issue of the pornography nor with the S & M abusive behavior. The wife viewed the affair as the *only* issue that she needed to deal with. Sadly, the husband was not willing to change his behavior.

Abuse

Physical, verbal, and even financial abuses in the home are all equal opportunity destroyers. Neglect and abandonment would also fall under this category. The father is responsible for keeping his family safe and protected, but when he is the source of harm, his family needs to leave to another safe place of covering, or the abuser needs to be removed. First Peter 3:7 clearly indicates that a husband's prayers and fellowship with God are hindered when he mistreats his wife. Remember, even our earthly relationships have a spiritual dynamic. Every time a husband chooses to use his strength, power and authority against his wife, instead of for her benefit, his heart is further hardened against the Holy Spirit, and sinful attitudes are further solidified in his character (Shaffer 2005).

Children who live in the home of an abusive coverer, witnessing abusive attitudes and behaviors, are impacted in many ways. They might experience fearfulness, bitterness, low self-esteem, post-traumatic stress, and spiritual confusion, to name a few. It is common for abused female children to get involved with abusive men later in life and for male children to become abusers themselves. When Jesus said that causing a child to sin was an offense worthy of death, (Matt. 18:6; Luke 17:2) was He merely being dramatic or does such a drastic punishment reveal how grave the offense is in the eyes of our Lord? (Shaffer 2005).

Consider the horrible stories of abuse that occurred by convicted child abuser Jerry Sandusky. He was a football coach at Pennsylvania State University for many years and led an organization for under privileged children. He was accused and then convicted in 2012 of many occurrences of child sexual abuse over several years. He used his influence and position to abuse children. The children trusted him and expected him to care for them. He did not. The young people were supposed to be safe and secure. They were not. His evil selfishness caused many lives to be destroyed, caused a well-respected football program to be shaken, and caused many university officials and fellow coaches to be fired or forced to resign. When what Sandusky, as a coach and a perceived caregiver, did in darkness and secret came into the light, the fallout was great and ruined many lives.

Church leaders, pastors, and priests have been called out and convicted of sexual and physical abuse over the last several years. A house of worship is supposed to be a place of safety and refuge for hurting souls. Churches are the ultimate places of covering for many people. When ministers take advantage of hurting people, causing deeper hurt, they no longer are safe caregivers, but victimizers. Lives are damaged and ruined instead of being healed and restored.

As mentioned earlier, verbal abusers are violent controllers. Instead of using physical force like physical abusers, they use words as weapons. Words that are demeaning, harsh, blaming, and attacking eventually wear down the victim creating fear, guilt, and shame in the victim. Once again, I invoke Proverbs 15:4: "A soothing tongue is a tree of life, but perversion in it crushes the spirit." A coverer, in contrast, looks to encourage and affirm those for whom he is responsible. The truth is that a coverer gains his wife's and his family's devotion because of his servant leadership approach, while an abuser will lose his family. A coverer establishes peace in the home, while an abuser creates turmoil and chaos.

Finally, financial abuse has been a growing issue in families. Financial abuse takes on different forms. The first and most common is when, usually the husband, tightly controls the money and makes all decisions without communicating with his wife. The wife is often unaware of financial issues such as life insurance, financial investments, and retirement plans. The husband typically does not welcome the wife's input in any financial matters. He may ask for his wife's paycheck and then give her only an "allowance" to limit her spending. This is not the same as living within an agreed upon budget. Rather, the husband is treating his wife like a child.

Another way financial abuse plays out is requiring the wife to account for *literally* every penny that she spends. This often carries over to "time abuse" when the husband requires the wife to account for every minute of her day or tells her how to conduct her day. Instead of feelings of support, empowerment, and competence, there is only fear, guilt, humiliation, and shame (Shaffer 2005).

There are also instances where the children and the employed wife are taking care of or "bailing out" the husband because of irresponsible financial behaviors. This can be a result of the mentality among some men that their wives, for instance, are supposed to "take care" of them. Sometimes, the grown children are required to help. Second Corinthians 12:14 says, "For children are not responsible to save up for their parents, but parents for their children." This has become a common theme among many men today.

Divorce

Divorce has become so easy these days that one in two marriages ends in divorce. That is true both in the mainstream *and* in the church. For example, in Connecticut, divorce is routinely granted about ninety days after one spouse files the necessary papers, with no reason needed. If an individual represents himself, it may coast him only $225-$250 (Kupelian 2005). When a husband has divorced his wife, he does not stop becoming responsible for his children. Stepfathers may become the household covering, but I believe God still holds the biological father accountable for his children, their ultimate well-being, and ultimate outcome. Good stepfathers can stand in the gap and become a responsible coverer, which is the proper thing to do, but how the biological father originally conducted himself with regards to his responsibilities and his family, will be what he is accountable for. The fact that he is the father does not end when he leaves the home, no matter how hard he tries to run from this.

A divorce affects the family for years to come. Wallerstein (2000) has shown over a twenty-five year study that children from divorced and remarried families experience more depression, have more learning difficulties, and suffer from more problems with peers than children from intact families suffer. She indicates that children from these homes are two to three times more likely to be referred for psychological help at school than their peers from intact families.

More of them end up in mental health clinics and hospital settings. There is earlier sexual activity, more children born out of wedlock, less marriage and more divorce among children coming from divorced homes (Wallerstein 2000).

In addition, Stephen Baskerville (2003), a professor of political science at Howard University, concluded that virtually the major personal and social pathologies could be traced to fatherlessness more than to any other single factor. Citing violent crime, substance abuse, unwed pregnancy, suicide, and other problems, he observed that fatherlessness far surpasses both poverty and race as a predictor of social deviance (Baskerville 2003). In every state, the portion of families where children have two parents, rather than one, has dropped significantly over the past decade. "Fifteen million U.S. children, or 1 in 3, live without a father. In 1960, just 11 percent of American children lived in homes without fathers" (Liberty Alliance, 2012). Gentlemen, we are responsible for our children, whether we are living with them or not. The outcome and well-being of our children are at stake. As men, we need to do better putting our own desires aside, and humbly provide for and cover our children.

Miscellaneous

There are other pursuits or habits that men need to reform in their lives. Psalms 115:4–8 states that we become that which we pursue. "Their idols are silver and gold, the work of man's hands ... Those who make them *will become like them*, everyone who trusts in them" (Italics mine). This is the essence of idolatry. It is therefore imperative that we pursue Christ, in order to be like Him (Rom. 1:23–25; 1 John 3:1–10). Our children and wives are watching. Our fellow employees are watching. Our fellow brothers and sisters in the Lord are watching. You can believe that the world is definitely watching.

Men often set the tone for their homes and businesses. There is a saying in the corporate world that goes something like this: "It comes down from the top." That is so true. For example, when we are driving, are we quick to lambaste another driver for cutting us off? Or can we control our tongue and simply use that as an object lesson for one of our children, a future potential driver? We *are* being watched.

How is our language? Do we speak at home the same way we speak at church? Do we speak in the work place in a vulgar manner, because others do it? Men, we are leaders. We *are* being watched.

What television shows do we watch and tolerate? Shows like *The Simpsons, Family Guy, Two and a Half Men*, and *Will and Grace* are insidious in the demeaning of family life and sexual messages. What type of violent shows do we watch? The so-called "reality shows" portray a limited and demented reality of some, but not the reality that needs to be exemplified in our lives. Even watching sports on television can be a maneuvering challenge due to the commercials. Do we attempt to flip the channel when something offensive is in view? We *are* being watched.

Do we make lewd remarks about women when we think no one else is around? Do our eyes wander? Do we make remarks about our bosses or supervisors that shows disrespect? We *are* being watched.

What kind of temper do we exhibit? Are we quick to fly off the handle, or can we recover quickly and see situations for what they are? Is self-control a fruit of the Spirit in our life? Inner strength is so much more powerful than trying to be a "macho" man. Proverbs 16:32 says, "He who is slow to anger is better than the mighty, and he who rules his spirit, than he who captures a city." We *are* being watched.

Are we making excuses and blaming others when things go

wrong? Can we be man enough to admit when we are wrong? The lie is that if we *admit* that we failed or wronged someone, it is a sign of weakness. The *truth* is that in being honest and taking responsibility, we operate from a standpoint of strength. When God addressed Job, He declared, "Now gird up your loins like a man" (38:3, 40:7). Even when we admit we are wrong to our children, in reality, this is a sign of strength and it is a wonderful relationship builder. We *are* being watched.

How do we treat our bodies? Are we gluttons and couch potatoes? Do we *speak* of the evils of excess but live selfishly and in self-gratification? Do we live with habits that are damaging to our health, like smoking and drug or alcohol abuse? Do we exercise? We *are* being watched.

All of these and more are just small areas over which we can take control and show levels of leadership that can affect our lives and so many others around us. God can equip us with strength of heart and mind. Second Timothy 1:7 says, "For God hath not given us the spirit of fear; but of power, and of love, and of a sound mind" (KJV).

We *are* being watched! "For the eyes of the Lord move to and fro throughout the earth that He may strongly support those whose heart is completely His" (2 Chron. 16:9). Our children are watching us as well. So are our spouses. So are our family members. Being an example is not easy, and none of us will ever be perfect. However, if we submit to the Coverer of our souls, we can be assured that He is conforming us to His image.

It is without question that once the man is "taken out," the family is adversely affected, which in turn affects the community and culture. The devil's strategy is to go after the head because he knows if he is successful, there is a ripple effect for years to come. The devil will either try to remove the covering completely or deceive the covering into following after destructive behaviors, such as addictions or abuse. Either way, the results are similar.

As I noted in chapter 3, the movie *The Patriot* provides a scene that underscores this strategy. Benjamin Martin and General Cornwallis were engaged in a dialog about the rules of war. The conversation in this scene focused on the "taking out" of the officers in a battle. Cornwallis tried to appeal to Martin to refrain from targeting the officers or leaders as it would lead to chaos on the battlefield. Satan has the same tactic. If the devil can be successful in "taking out" or hindering the effectiveness of men, then families, communities, churches, and societies can adversely be impacted. The devil is after the head. He even tried to "take out" Jesus, but was ultimately defeated through Jesus' stand against temptation and later, His resurrection (Matt. 4:1–11; Luke 4:1–13).

In biblical history, it is recording that Satan attempted to target men, who are called to be the covering for their families. Ultimately and in particular, he was seeking to break the Messianic bloodline. In the Old Testament, Pharaoh decreed such a command to the midwives of the nation. Exodus 1:16, 22 says,

> When you are helping the Hebrew women to give birth and see them upon the birthstool, if it is a son, then you shall put him to death; but if it is a daughter, then she shall live … Every son who is born you are cast into the Nile, and every daughter you are to keep alive.

After Moses was born, his mother hid him and then placed him a basket and floated the basket down the Nile. Pharaoh's daughter rescued Moses, and as a result, the Hebrew deliver was saved.

In the New Testament, male children were once again targeted, this time by King Herod. The Messiah had been born, and the Magi came to honor him. Instead of returning to Herod to inform him where the child had been located, Herod issued a decree. Matthew 2:16 says,

> Then when Herod saw that he had been tricked by the magi, he became very enraged, and sent and slew all the male children who were in Bethlehem and all its vicinity, from two years old and under, according to the time which he had determined from the magi.

This was a direct attempt to kill all the male children, specifically to destroy the Messiah, humankind's ultimate covering. Both of these accounts indicate the spiritual warfare that occurs against God's purposes. Satan's desire is to indeed "take out" or deceive the men of every culture. If successful, families and cultures are negatively affected.

The good news is that Satan does not have to win. He could not remove Jesus as our covering, despite his efforts in the wilderness and on the cross. Jesus withstood the onslaught on the earth and under the earth, through His victorious resurrection. It is only through Christ that we can hope to see restored "coverings" in our homes, in our communities and in our societies.

CHAPTER 7
How to Restore the Covering

God's design has no flaws. Adam's behavior caused an opening in the "hedge," and sin and evil influence walked right on in to harass relationships and the family. The hope rests now on the "Last Adam" (1 Cor. 15:45), Jesus Christ, and His shed blood and His finished work. He made it possible for us to be restored in relationship with God, then with each other, and finally to the original design. But it is an ongoing battle. The victory is sure, however, but we need to *fight* for peace.

When a covering has been damaged or destroyed, there are several ways to restore it. The first is to make an absolute firm decision as to whom you are going to serve. Even Bob Dylan, one of the more influential poets of the 1960s, '70s, and '80s, wrote, that you have to serve somebody (Columbia Records 1979). Since it is true that men are not without a covering, we need to decide if we are going to submit, or come under, God, or are we going to submit to earthly influences and self-centered agendas.

In the true sense of the word, there really is no such thing as an atheist. While an atheist is either anti-God or he believes that God does not exist, he is still submitting to *something* that guides and influences his life. Essentially, whatever controls us, is a god to us. Jesus said, "For where your treasure is, there your heart will be also" (Matt. 6:21). We *all* serve whatever the most important thing is in our lives. Matthew 12:35 states, "The good man brings out of his good treasure what is good; and the evil man brings out of his evil treasure what is evil."

As coverers, we respond to what is important to us. So, first, the question we are to ask ourselves is, who will be our covering? Will it be the ways and deceptions of the world and the devil? Or will we submit to God, the One we can truly count on to guide us into His benefits and into a peace that passes all understanding? Gentlemen, it is really in our best interest that we accept Jesus Christ and come under His covering. As a result, our decision to do so will set us free to cover as God designed it. We will see God empower us to make a positive difference.

Joshua declared:

> Now, therefore, fear the Lord and serve Him in sincerity and truth; and put away the gods which your fathers served beyond the River and in Egypt, and serve the Lord. If it is disagreeable in your sight to serve the Lord, choose for yourselves today whom you will serve: whether the gods which your fathers served which were beyond the River, or the gods of the Amorites in whose land you are living; but as for me and my house, we will serve the Lord. (Josh. 24:14–15)

It is simply not enough to be "religious" and yet dead in our iniquity. Joshua made it clear that *he and his house* would serve God. His house would follow his lead. He believed his influence would be passed down to the rest of his family. His decision would also impact his effectiveness in other areas of his responsibilities and of his world. Joshua was acknowledging that his ability to cover was based upon choosing to be covered by God.

Marriage is not simply a love and commitment issue. It is a faith issue. Eggerichs writes:

> Whatever I do for my spouse, I do it for Christ as well. A husband's unconditional love for his wife reveals his love for Christ. The husband who loves God should love his wife also. If you are not loving your wife, then you must ask yourself, "Am I really loving Jesus Christ?" A wife's unconditional respect for her husband reveals her reverence for Christ (Eph. 5:21-22; 6:6–7). The wife who respects God should respect her husband. If you are not respecting your husband, then you must ask yourself, "Am I really loving Jesus Christ?" (Eggerichs 2004).

Sacrificial love brings safety and security to women and children. Respect and peace bring safety and security to men. Feeling safe encourages the continuation of sacrifice in relationships and allows faith to grow. Growing faith often encourages individuals towards creative expressions and endeavors, and even towards taking positive risks.

As men, we are first to submit to God, our covering—the only resource that will never fail us! Submitting to God means that we are to follow His ways and do what is right. When we do that, we will see our families respond with respect and the willingness to submit to us. Our families will know that we can be trusted. Trust occurs when we believe that someone else has *our* best interest in mind. We can believe that about God. Our families need to believe that about *us*.

Another way to restore the covering is for men to intercede for their family members and the direction of their family itself. Too often in churches, the "intercessory prayer" groups are comprised almost entirely of women. Also, "researchers have found that adolescent girls are more religious than are adolescent boys (King & Roeser 2009). Gentlemen, we should be ashamed of this. While we can be thankful that faithful women do pray for others, their church, their pastor, their families, etc., God desires to hear from men as coverers. Women are good at intercessory prayer, for intercessory prayer is prayer for others. Men need to intercede for their families as well, and not just leave it up to their wives. Women know that they need a covering. Men need to be taught that they need a covering as well. Can you picture the famous painting of General George Washington kneeling on snowy ground in prayer? It is a powerful painting to reflect upon, especially as we have learned of Washington's integrity, humility, and influence during the early stages of our nation. This man of prayer made a difference! I believe if men were to pray, we would witness the power of God in a life-changing way, in our families, churches, and communities. Why? Because we are called to be coverers!

Of the many examples in Scripture, the life of Job is an excellent model for all coverers. The Bible describes Job as a man who was "blameless, upright, fearing God, and turning away from evil" (Job 1:1). Job's family and possessions are then described, and he is clearly seen as a blessed and influential man (Job 1: 3). His family regularly feasted together and apparently blessed each other (Job 1:4). This family shows all the signs of a special group of people. Yet Job regularly did a very interesting thing: "When the days of feasting had completed their cycle, Job would send and consecrate them, rising up early in the morning and offering burnt offerings according to the number of them all; for Job said, 'Perhaps my sons sinned and cursed God in their hearts.' Thus Job did *continually* [italics added]"

(Job 1:5). Incredibly, this man prayed and interceded for his entire family, making provision for them with regards to redemption and forgiveness of their sins. Evidently, he did this often enough to have made a difference in the lives of his family members.

Contrast Job's example with many coverers today who neglect their families, abuse their families, invite iniquity into their families, and simply destroy their families. Job's success and reputation is absolutely related to his willingness to first cover his family. Most men want to stand out from the crowd and make an impact. It is how our Creator wired us. However, men often choose to go about this the wrong way. God will bring the increase, as we show faithfulness in our responsibilities. As shown by Jesus, He will indeed give more to those who can be responsible with little. Essentially, it starts in the home. If we can be good, responsible coverers in the home, God will expand our tents!

Years ago, when I was a manager of a retail store, my district manager came to make his monthly visit one day and proceeded to tell me that I did not work enough hours. We were required to work forty-five to fifty hours per week, and I consistently worked forty-five to fifty hours per week. Yet most of my peers worked fifty to seventy hours per week. I remember our conversation sounded something like this:

> "Bob, you need to be in the store more."
> "With all due respect, Mike, am I missing my dead-
>   lines?"
> "Well, no."
> "Am I completing the merchandising early or on time?"
> "Well, yes."
> "Are my employees taking care of our customers?"
> "Well, yes."
> "Am I up to date with our shipping and receiving?"

"Yes. Your back room is neater than the rest of my stores."

"Is my store meeting the budgeted sales goals?"

"Well, yes. You are running 11 percent above plan."

"Then, when I am finished with my day, I will go home. I consider the real measure of my success first, how my family turns out, and I need to be there for them. The rest will come."

"You know, I wish my brother-in-law would be more attentive to his family. His kids are …"

He then proceeded to tell me about his sister's family who was in chaos because of turmoil in the home, due to, among other things, his brother-in-law being a workaholic and struggling with an additional addiction.

A third way to restore the covering is simply to do what Job did. The above quoted verse indicated that Job turned "away from evil." (Job 1:1). This "turning away" is a vigilant, run-from-with-all-your-might type of action. This approach deals with many things. For example, if the husband has a pornography problem or addiction, then he should vigilantly run from and destroy any connection to it as soon as possible. If he is struggling with such an drastic approach, then perhaps he should courageously consider Christian counseling in order to obtain healing for the pain and hurt in his life. Also, he should *run* from all the trappings of pornography. If he has magazines and videos, he can have a "cleansing party" by *burning* them all at once. What better way to destroy this evil than by letting it burn! If he has used the Internet, then strong filters can be obtained, or even better, the drastic and effective method of simply disconnecting the Internet may be needed.

Often, vigilance is called for and is required. Men need to do what Job did, and that was to make a "covenant with his eyes" (Job

31:1), not to gaze upon another woman. Essentially, pornography can be a hatred of women, as mentioned earlier, and a man cannot be an effective coverer if such feelings exist. The exploitation of women and the desire to harm women needs to be eradicated from the spirit of men. Only God can restore that which was stolen and destroyed, namely, the love and desire to cover the woman and daughters in the life of that husband and father.

If the husband has an issue with abuse and anger, then he too perhaps needs Christian counseling or deliverance, and the family may need to escape to a safe place for a time. The husband is in desperate need of seeing restored to him things that were not provided while he was a youngster, and that may take time. Through therapy and a relationship with Jesus, he may need (1) to experience the *unconditional* love he may have never had, (2) the empowerment to be under control and responsible, (3) to learn how to express forgiveness and give up his "right" for vengeance, and (4) to have his hurts healed once and for all. I have heard it said many times that hurt people, hurt people. Marriage intervention and counseling may also be needed since the wife's and children's safety is to be secured.

If such abuse or neglect relates to a drinking or a drug problem, again, vigilance will be needed. A completely turning away from this destructive habit will be necessary. Counseling and accountability groups often help with the substance addiction. A healing touch from God will be necessary as well, for both the physical dependency and the emotional hurt. If alcohol or drugs were in the home, then activities such as pouring alcohol down the drain or flushing them down the toilet provides an effective visual cleansing. Smashing the bottles and burning the drugs in a controlled environment can also be effect ways of making the statement that these evils are no longer invited to be part of the home.

The bottom line is that any evil in the form of harmful behavior, any evil in the form of addictive vices, and anything that places the family in jeopardy, should be changed, tossed out, destroyed, and removed from the home. Coverers provide a model, and the children will often adopt that model for their lives as well. Exodus 34:6–7 says:

> The Lord, the Lord God, compassionate and gracious, slow to anger, and abounding in lovingkindness and truth; who keeps lovingkindness for thousands, who forgives iniquity, transgressions and sin; yet He will by no means leave the guilty unpunished, visiting the iniquity of *fathers* [emphasis added] on the children and on the grandchildren to the third and fourth generations.

God is gracious to forgive and change our lives, but iniquity will be passed down to future generations through the fathers. If *sins* of the fathers can torment third and fourth generations, so, too, do *wounds* of the fathers (Tauke 2004). The break in the hedge can be repaired and restored to strength. It is up to the husband/father to do that when it happens.

As I mentioned earlier, my dad was a third generation alcoholic. Thanks be to God that I did not follow that same path. However, I had to be aware of not just my convictions, but my behavior as well. Our children would hear about the evils of drinking and would often see it in the lives of others in the family. A couple of times, early in our marriage, I would purchase a bottle of wine to celebrate our wedding anniversary together. I thought, no harm done; one time a year … Then once, when one of our older sons was about nine years old, he noticed the wine bottle in the refrigerator and questioned me about it. I tried to explain it away as a once a year, legitimate celebration. My son said, "I thought you felt strongly about alcohol,

Dad?" I then realized the message I was giving my children was not consistent with my convictions. As a result, I gladly disposed of the wine and the bottle.

Since then, my wife and I were quite happy in celebrating our anniversary with "sparkling apple cider," and our kids can even join us! Our adult children have watched our lifestyle over the years and know today that alcohol is not to be a prominent part of one's life. Even though my wife and I can enjoy a glass of wine from time to time, it is not a consistent part of our lifestyle. This is not legalism. This is freedom. Freedom is *not* the *ability* to do what we want. Again, freedom is the *power* to do what is right! To be under a covering grants us this power. Freedom is empowerment. It is *not* independence. God did not create us to be independent, but to walk in freedom, as we depend on Him! God empowers us to be free. However, we cannot do so independent of God.

Finally, the book of Nehemiah provides an excellent blueprint towards restoration and changing behaviors. Nehemiah 9:2-3 says, "The descendants of Israel separated themselves ... and stood and confessed their sins and the iniquity of their fathers. While they stood in their place, they read from the book of the Law of the Lord their God ... and worshiped the Lord their God." Because we are ultimately in a spiritual war, a return to true worship of our God and responsible confession of our sins and hurts are the foundation to Nehemiah's plan. Tauke (2004) calls it "Nehemiah's Family-Legacy Recovery Formula." There are four steps to consider:

1. Confess sins of fathers: Acknowledge historic family wounds.

2. Assess impact of family failure: Make clear value judgments and assign responsibility.

3. Chronicle or list overlooked or underrated family heroes, victories, and achievements—often disregarded or down-graded as victims, these individuals wallow in family pain.

4. Lean heavily on personal responsibility and divine guidance for an escape hatch from chronic and debilitating family habits.

Family wounds and generational curses are important aspects to identify.

The power of Christ can eradicate such bondages, so that the individual can chart a new course of freedom. For example, abuse and alcoholism are examples of behaviors that are passed down from generation to generation. Personal responsibility for our actions should lead us to Jesus for forgiveness, restoration, and renewal, all of which are essential to be an effective coverer.

Since men are called to be responsible coverers, we need to be ever mindful of our responsibility before God to be corrected, to be *courageous* to admit wrongfulness and iniquity, and to look to be restored under the loving and empowering covering of our Lord. Correction is not the same as criticism. Repentance is not weakness. Being contrite will create an atmosphere of safety, for someone who is willing to admit wrong, becomes real and approachable.

Sometimes, a woman can restore the covering by simply honoring and respecting her husband more. In his book, *Love and Respect*, Dr. Emerson Eggerichs writes, "Something in a man longs for his wife to look up to him as he fulfills this role. And when she does, it motivates him, not because he is arrogant, but because of how God has constructed him" (Eggerichs 2004, 53). While women need unconditional love, men need unconditional respect (Eggerichs 2004). God designed interaction between a husband and wife, to be a thing of beauty and satisfaction. Ladies, if you honor and respect your husbands, you will find that they in turn will provide the love you desire and need. The reverse is also true. Men do not need to concentrate on *changing* their spouses. Rather they need to focus on loving their wives. Women cannot expect to *change* their husbands. Rather, they need to focus on respecting their men, and usually good things will happen.

There are women who desire to be in control and who do not want their husbands to lead. This is out of balance, and the wife has essentially come out from her covering. "The deepest yearning of their hearts—for love—is clouded by negativity" (Eggerichs 2004, 88). Our society has taught young girls and women to be independent. Again, Eggerichs writes,

> There are voices in our culture that have been saying, "Don't show respect to men; they don't deserve it. They'll treat you in a subservient way, or they'll abuse you and even kill you." This is true of a certain number of men, but I believe it is a lie concerning the vast majority.

However, as mentioned earlier, no one has been created to be independent—neither men nor women. In reality, a wife has more influence with her husband than she often thinks, provided she has the right attitude. A woman's call is to "quietly receive instruction with entire submissiveness" (1 Tim. 2:11). Also, "Wives, be submissive to your own husbands so that even if any of them are disobedient to the word, they may be won without a word by the behavior of their wives, as they observe your chaste and respectful behavior" (1 Peter 3:1–2). To build up your husband with honor, respect, and positive regard means to strengthen the covering of love that a wife desires anyway.

One time, I had a confrontation with my teenage daughter in the presence of my wife. Honestly, I made a big deal out of nothing, upsetting my daughter. My wife knew that I was wrong. When I sought her out for affirmation, she simply said that she did not understand what the conflict was all about. The next day it truly dawned on me that I was wrong and had over-reacted. I bought flowers and came home to give them to my daughter, asking for her forgiveness. She did forgive me. I then went to my wife, and I let her know that I appreciated her posture, even though I realized she knew all along that I had acted like a buffoon. I believe this type of scenario can happen more often when the wife leaves her husband in God's hands. He is pretty good at getting our attention!

Ultimately, we need to understand that nothing we do is outside of God's view. We can never be successful in our attempts to run and hide. Men who spend so much time and energy pursuing sin and running from God, will find little, if any, rest. Job 34: 21–22 says, "For His eyes are upon the ways of a man, and He sees all his steps. There is no darkness or deep shadow where the workers of iniquity may hide themselves." Gentlemen, come back under the covering, and you will find protection, peace, purpose, and freedom.

CHAPTER 8
As It Should Be: A Summary

Ladies and gentleman, the stakes are high! Business as usual in the church is over. Radical changes are needed in the way in which we conduct ourselves, guide our families, and fulfill our responsibilities. It does not take much today to appear different, but that is what's required. The world is against the ways of God. Indeed, some *churches* are against the ways and power of God. All creation is crying out for God's design, man, to be covered by Him and to be responsible coverers of his loved ones and responsibilities.

We have seen that God designed man to be His steward; for women to be an equal-in-value helpmate and partner who is loved, protected, and cherished by her man; for children to be protected, trained, mentored, and prepared for adult life, primarily by the father; and for the man's legacy to have a positive impact for many generations to come. Psalm 78:5–7 says:

> He commanded our *fathers* (italics added), that they should teach … their children, that the generation to come might know, even the children yet to be born … that they should

put their confidence in God and not forget the works of
God, but keep His commandments ...

We have learned, through Scriptural examples, attitudes, and
behaviors that were both pleasing and displeasing to God, and the
corresponding results of each. We have seen how God deals with and
calls men directly, but also how Satan directly attacks men through
habits, deception, and self-centeredness.

- As the Great Coverer, God desires to teach and equip:
- "I will instruct you and teach you in the way which
  you should go; I will counsel you with my eye upon
  you." (Ps. 32:8).
- "But the Helper, the Holy Spirit, whom the Father will
  send in my name, He will teach you all things, and
  bring to your remembrance all that I said to you." (John
  14:26).

- As men, we need to come under our Great Coverer:
- "Teach me Your way, O Lord, and lead me in a level path."
  (Ps. 27:11).
- "Teach me Your way, O Lord; I will walk in Your truth;
  Unite my heart to fear Your name." (Ps. 86:11).
- "How blessed is the man who fears the Lord, who greatly
  delights in His commandments." (Ps. 112:1).
- "Give instruction to a wise man and he will be wiser,
  teach a righteous man and he will increase his learning."
  (Prov. 9:9).

- For children, this should be the posture:
- "Hear, my son, you father's instruction and do not forsake
  your mother's teaching." (Prov. 1:8).
- "Hear, O sons, the instruction of a father, and give attention that you may gain understanding." (Prov. 4:1).
- "A wise son accepts his father's discipline, but a scoffer does
  not listen to rebuke." (Prov. 13:1).

- "Children, obey your parents in the Lord, for this is right. "Honor your father and mother," which is the first commandment with promise: "that it may go well with you and you may live long on the earth." (Eph. 6:1-3).

To all the wives: remember your husband in your daily prayers. He is the "point man" and receives all kinds of fiery darts from the devil, every day. Honor him and look to him for your covering, for it will benefit you and your relationship with him. He is not just your head and leader; he needs your support to follow through with responsible behavior. You do have a voice, and it is a voice of love, respect, and empowerment. Proverbs 12:4 says, "An excellent wife is the crown of her husband, But she who shames him is like rottenness in his bones." He may truly want to do what is right, but you may need to give up control and your desire to manipulate.

Among the many attributes of a fine woman in Proverbs 31:10–31, is that her husband, "trusts in her" (v. 11) and he "praises her saying: 'Many daughters have done nobly, but you excel them all'" (v. 28–29). Can your husband say this about you? Again, to have trust is simply to believe that someone else has *your* best interest at heart. Do you have your husband's best interest in mind? Husbands, do you have your wife's best interest in mind? If trust exits, safety and security is an important by-product. Self-centeredness has no place in a good, strong, and intimate relationship. Proverbs 25:24 gives a poignant word picture: "It is better to live in a corner of the roof, than in a house with a contentious woman." For the man, Proverbs 29:23 provides a promise: "A man's pride will bring him low, but a humble spirit will obtain honor."

The desire to control has to be surrendered, without a doubt. For the husband, the call and responsibility is covering, not controlling. For the wife, controlling her husband weakens him, and in turn, places her in jeopardy. A wise woman would seek to avoid such vulnerability. Proverbs 14:1 says, "The wise woman builds her house, but the foolish tears it down with her own hands." It is indeed ironic that any attempts to control actually leads to the weakening of the bond in any relationship. Once that bond weakens, the relationship is ripe for attacks from the devil. If conflicts and anger linger in a relationship, we have allowed the devil the opportunity to wreak havoc in that relationship (Eph. 4:27).

In 1 Timothy 3:1–13 and Titus 1:5–9, we read about requirements for men who are aspiring to be leaders, deacons and elders in the church. These same descriptions can help men understand what God desires in overseers and coverers in general. Titus 1:6–11 particularly speaks to this:

> If any man is above reproach, the husband of one wife, having children who believe, not accused of dissipation (drunkenness) or rebellion. For the overseer must be above reproach as God's steward, not self-willed, not quick-tempered, not addicted to wine, not pugnacious, not fond of sordid gain, but hospitable, loving what is good, sensible, just, devout, self-controlled, holding fast the faithful word which is in accordance with the teaching, so that he will be able both to exhort in sound doctrine and to refute those who contradict. For there are many rebellious men, empty talkers and deceivers, especially those of the circumcision, who must be silenced because they are upsetting whole families, teaching things they should not teach for the sake of sordid gain.

Notice how overseers are described as "God's stewards." He is still the owner, but He chooses simply to dispatch men to be *responsible* coverers. The word "sordid" means, "morally degrading." This can be an appropriate description of pornography and sexual abuse. "So husbands ought also to love their own wives as their own bodies. He who loves his own wife loves himself" (Eph. 5:28).

I find it interesting that God would desire to "silence" men who would disrupt and upset families. God will indeed deal directly with men, in both a just and loving manner. Yet God's intent is for men to live as coverers that are described as good, devout, self-controlled, etc. The Lord sees all that we do and knows all that we think, and yet He desires to provide us with whatever we need to be a changed, successful coverer. I have come to rest in the fact that God wants me to be successful in whatever I put my hands to. That rest comes from the realization that I cannot do anything without Him. Yet at the same time, as Paul confessed, "I can do all things through Him who strengthens me" (Phil. 4:13).

The battles that we fight today are, first and foremost, spiritual warfare. The forces of evil are against God, His design and His people. This is especially true with regards to the family and relationships. Scripture reminds us that we war not against flesh and blood, "but against the world forces of this darkness, against the spiritual forces of wickedness in the heavenly places" (Eph. 6:12). The roles of men and women have been distorted so much so that *increased* evil has been allowed to have access to our families. As it was shown earlier in this book, there is a "top-down" effect. If Satan deceives the men, then families, communities, regions, and nations will be affected as well. The good news is that the tide can turn, by the blood of Christ, which covers us.

So, our battle cry should be: "The name of the Lord is a strong tower; the righteous runs into it and is safe" (Prov. 18:10). Men, let us call upon the name of our Lord, worship Him, come under his covering, as He is our strong tower, and be strengthened and protected. Then, and only then, can we expect to see the fruitfulness of our efforts to cover our wives, our children, and our responsibilities. Remember, God has to separate light from darkness. Let us allow Him to do so in our lives!

I take seriously the position I have when I counsel individuals and couples and when I speak at conferences. I understand that God has placed me in this influential position. I realize that those who come are dear ones to God. So, I start every day with this prayer: "Lord, thank you for this responsibility and privilege. I cannot do this without You. I do not *want* to do this without You. Help me see what You see, know what You know, hear what You hear, and speak only what You would have me say to these dear ones. I ask for Your anointing and covering, so that I can be effective. Thank You, Father. In Jesus' name ..."

I would like to encourage husbands, fathers, and any man who is responsible for his life, to seek God, speak prayers of repentance, devotion to and dependence upon your Heavenly Father who covers. Submit to Him and ask Him to change your life, behaviors, and attitudes. Look to care for your own and not to be taken care of. The days of being "parented" by our earthly parents do come to an end. Your heavenly Father, who is our eternal, loving parent, is quite capable of being there for you. That is His job. He desires to care for you and equip you. You *will* see a difference, not only in your life, but also in those for whom you are responsible.

To the wives and young people, honor your man and see him as God's gift to you. Some young people and adult children might say, "But you have no idea what my dad/mom did to me." Some dads have indeed been less than nurturing and very hurtful. However, forgiveness is essential in order for individuals to move forward in liberty. Forgiveness often benefits the forgiver more than the one who is in need of forgiveness. Forgiveness essentially *releases* the offender from the power to hurt the individual who was wounded.

On the other hand, perhaps children have dishonored their parents. In doing so, they have become contentious with their covering, behavior for which they are accountable. The commandment to honor your father and your mother is the only one that contains a promise: "for it will be well with you, and you will live long on the earth" (Eph. 6:1–3). Despising, cutting off, and dishonoring parents remove you from your covering and this will adversely affect you. Rosenbaum states:

> Making peace with our parents begins, not with forgiving their sins against us, but by asking their forgiveness for our sins against them. A lifetime of mistrust and anger towards parents unconsciously affects careers, other relationships, financial stability, and even our health and sense of worth. By seeking God's guidance in keeping the commandment to honor our father and mother, which Paul called "the first commandment with a promise," we can take the first liberating steps toward building new relationships with our parents, family, friends—and with ourselves. (Rosenbaum 1994, from the book cover)

The way we treat our parents will also carry over to how we conduct our relationship with God. Chances are that if you contend with and despise parents, you will contend with and despise God. The ability to know that God has good intentions and security in store for you is impeded by the dishonoring of our parents.

For those who have had parents who were good, but still less than ideal, pray for them daily, as they are pummeled daily by the fiery darts of the devil and the forces of the world. Men and women are wired to be doers, and many want to do what is right. We are called to build each other up. Empowered fathers and mothers can be good and responsible coverers.

Single Parents

For women who are without a husband because of death, incarceration, divorce, addictions in the man, and abandonment, they become the coverings over their families. The Scriptures are clear that such women need to be covered by the grace of God. There are alternatives to seek for a covering over themselves and their families. First, as in the case of Hagar, there is God Himself, who sees and promises to look after such families. Also, Ruth made the choice to follow the God of the Hebrews, instead of returning to her land to seek out another husband. This lesson is critical because many women seek another husband instead of seeking after God. To Ruth, "there was something more important than having a man beside her at night" (Evans 1995, 29). First Timothy 5:1–16 provides instruction for the care of widows and parents, and pious living as a single parent.

The Bible says: "The Lord preserves the strangers; He relieves the fatherless and widow" (Ps. 146:9). Also, Psalm 10:14 says, "Thou art the helper of the fatherless." Make God your covering, ladies, and He will empower you to lead in such a single parent home. Ladies, be strong in the Lord and not vulnerable to men who could become unhealthy husbands and fathers to you and your children. It is often better for a single mom to have no man than to have a bad man. This may often be a difficult decision, but please use discernment and not your vulnerable situation in order to seek a relationship. Look to the Father for protection and guidance and He will indeed cover you.

If you are a single mom, I would simply say to be careful with whom you are considering as a future husband. Often, a single mom can feel desperate in her circumstances. Often, a single mom is in a vulnerable state, and there are men out there who would take advantage of your situation. You could be like blood for sharks! In acting out of desperation, discernment could be ignored. Any man that you would consider needs to love you *and* your children. Do not allow anyone to be your covering who simply has an agenda of wanting to be with you, but not your children. Your children's safety could be at stake. Remember, God is a God who sees, and He knows your circumstances. Keep in mind the stories of Hagar and Ruth. Lean on the Lord and be guided by His wisdom, and you should be able to discern who, if anyone, would be best for you and your family.

Secondly, seek out extended family for assistance first. Perhaps young single mothers could return to their parents for covering. This is the teaching of Scripture: "If any woman who is a believer has dependent widows, she must assist them and the church must not be burdened, so that it may assist those who are widows indeed" (1 Timothy 5:16). The extended family is to be considered first as covering for widows and single parents. The family, which is designed by God to be the basis of all civilization, is the first line of defense for protection, guidance, and provision. This is true in many cultures today, but is not often seen in the United States; in fact, in our society, "we have a generation today that has been trained to go to the government" (Evans 1995, 50), before any other resource. The church is to be considered second, especially for "widows indeed" or women who have no extended family available to them. Pastor Tony Evans sums it up for single parents who need covering:

> The first thing you find out is what God has for you. You go to His Word. after that, you find out what support systems are in your nuclear or extended family. The, you go to the family of God. When all else fails, that is when the broader society helps out. I must say again, we mix God's order up ... In fact, they go to the government before they even fulfill their personal responsibilities ... (2 Thess. 3:10). (Evans 1995, 50)

Perhaps an able family member could provide covering for a single mother and her children. However, ladies, always look for a coverer, not a controller.

Thirdly, find a good church that will help provide a covering through the leadership and community. If there are no family options, then seek out a church that can cover you and help care for your children. Many churches have mentoring couples or families who can provide some "covering" to a "broken" family. Many churches have singles ministries, but I believe that a single person benefits more from being "adopted" into an existing family for covering. For young women, this provides protection and guidance. For young men, this can provide additional opportunities for mentoring and for developing responsibility by functioning within a family. For single moms, an "adopted" covering situation can be a tremendous benefit. It may prevent a vulnerable woman from marrying again as a result of her desperate situation. I believe churches can do more in this area, in developing coverings for the fatherless.

My wife and I have had the privilege of mentoring and covering some single young adults over the years. A few have expressed gratitude for the benefit of being part of a family that experienced discipline and love. One young man, who was in college at the time and older than all our children, and who now has a family of his own, wrote to me his thoughts a few years ago:

> I got to see a different way for a family to operate that was healthy and to be able to learn from it. My father was not a follower of Christ, and thus it was impossible for him to model a godly way of relating to my mother or for raising children. In being a part of your family, and having a sense of adoption, I really got to see it on an operational level. I had to be around enough to catch it. It opened the door for

me to have someone to be able to advise me in a healthy manner in the stages of life. Spending so much time with a healthy godly family helped me to be able to heal areas in my life, most of which I was not even aware of. I just know I am a healthier person. I got a sense of responsibility that I don't think would have developed so quickly had I not been a part of the family. As the youngest child (in his own family), never before had people really looked up to me, or even looked on me as an example. That's really why the youngest are often looked upon as spoiled and self-centered. Really, there is no reason for them not to be in many cases. But your kids, my "brothers and sisters" made me think of others in a new way. We went to movies, and for the first time I thought about the messages in movies. I could not drive just anyway, because I had my "siblings" in the car with me. I made promises to be at games and concerts, and I know that I needed to make good on them. I got a sense of support in a very practical manner. You were all there to celebrate with me when I graduated college, and to pray with me when my father had surgery. When the college ministry (at church) died, it was only those of us who were connected with families in the church who stayed around. It was important that after the dust settled, I was still connected. If there was more of an effort to connect those in that group to families, I know that more would still be at (church) today. I agree that it is the best manner to see growth of college students in their walk with God. I know that there are many other things God has done in me through this relationship, but I want to tell you how much I have appreciated it.

Conclusion

Human beings were created to have dominion and an impact. Men, this does not mean that we are to act like bouncers and drill sergeants. Our families are looking for coverers, not controllers. Our societies are looking for righteous and responsible leaders. What many societies, including ours, are getting in their men are immoral, abusive, self-centered, lazy, and indulgent men. Our families and cultures are crying out for men and women who are living a life that can be trusted. Only through Jesus Christ can we be redeemed to live a life devoted our original calling and God-given design. What I have come to love about God is that He is the "Great Orchestrator." We are to play our part, and practice and perform responsibly, as God continues to be the One we look to for direction and harmony. Let us live to be responsible, provide care and safety to those around us, and then watch our God expand our tents!

Dr. Paul Meier, a prominent Christian psychiatrist and counselor, has listed five factors that are consistently found in mentally healthy families. They are:

- Love
- Discipline
- Consistency
- Example
- A man at the head of the home (Meier 1998)

The first three essentially speak for themselves. The fourth factor relates to the fact that, "our children learn their behavior from us. In the end, *they do what we do* much more than what we say they should do" (Meier 1998). Finally, He has observed through research and experience that, "a domineering, smothering mother and a weak father lie at the root of the vast majority of mental illnesses in children" (Meier 1998). This would be especially true regarding *absent* fathers as well. An absent father provides no covering, therefore no guidance, no purpose, and no protection. Keep in mind that an abusive man is not an emotionally strong man, but is essentially weak and wounded, attempting to make up for areas in his life that are lacking. Gentlemen, the impact that God has designed for men is not to be taken lightly or ignored. Our wives, children, and cultures are depending on the design of God.

Remember, God started with a man. That man was to learn and move according to his covering. Acts 17:28 says, "For in Him we live and move and exist …" As a man operates, what he covers is affected accordingly. Gentlemen, God starts with us. He desires relationship with us, for the purpose of blessing not just us, but those we love and cover. God desires to provide us with safety and security. He has done so through the death and resurrection of His Son, Jesus Christ. Relationship with Jesus will equip us with what we need to be loving and protective coverers. This is an absolute honor!

We are called to be responsible with what belongs to God. This breeds safety and security for all involved. As we function in righteous responsibility, and as we grow in godly maturity, our families, our churches, our communities, and our nation will take notice and be transformed according to the design that God intended! Be teachable; be submissive; be holy; and ultimately, *be blessed!*

References

⸙

About.com: Alcoholism. 2009. "Crime and Alcohol." http://alcoholism. about.com/cs/costs/a/aa980415.htm. (Accessed August 22, 2009)

American Association of Christian Counselors (AACC). 2009. "Addiction and Recovery Counselor Training Program." AACC Weekly Web Saver advertisement. (Accessed November 17, 2009)

Alcoholism Information.com, 2012. Alcohol Statistics. World Wide Web. Accessed December 29, 2012.

Arterburn, Stephen and Meg J. Rinck. 2000. *Avoiding Mr. Wrong (And What to Do If You Didn't).* Thomas Nelson Publishers. Nashville, TN.

Baker, Elizabeth. 1991. *Wanting To Follow, Forced To Lead.* Tyndale House Publishers. Wheaton, IL.

Bardon, Edward, M.D. 1978. *The Sexual Arena and Women's Liberation.* Nelson-Hall Publishers. Chicago, IL.

Barnhouse, Donald Grey. 1965. *The Invisible War.* Zondervan Publishing House. Grand Rapids, MI.

Baskerville, Stephen. 2003. "Divorce as Revolution," *Salisbury Review*, Vol. 21, No. 4, Summer, 2003.

Beck, J. R. 2000. "Gender Role Attitudes in Christian Marital Therapy: Issues of Importance and Ethics. A Millennium Review and Preview," *Marriage and Family: A Christian Journal.* Vol. 3, 345–357.

Burns, Alisa and Cath Scott. 1994. *Mother-Headed Families and Why They Have Increased.* Erlbaum & Associates. Hillsdale, NJ.

Dylan, Bob. 1979. *Gotta Serve Somebody.* From the album, <u>Slow Train Coming</u>, Columbia Records.

Eggerichs, Dr. Emerson. 2004. *Love & Respect.* Integrity Publishing. Nashville, TN.

Eldredge, John. 2001. *Wild at Heart.* Thomas Nelson Publishers. Nashville, TN.

Evans, Tony. 1995. *Tony Evans Speaks Out on Single Parenting.* Moody Press. Chicago, IL.

Holy Bible, New American Standard Version. 1999. Zondervan Publishing House. Grand Rapids, MI.

Horn, Wade F. and Tom Sylvester. 2002. *Father Facts: Fourth Edition.* National Fatherhood Initiative. Gaithersburg, MD.

Iverson, Dick. 1979. *Principles of Family Life.* Bible Temple Publishing. Portland, OR.

Jayson, Sharon. 2004. "It's Time To Grow Up—Later". USA Today. Garnett Co., Inc. September 30, 2004. <u>http://usatoday30.usatoday.com/life/lifestyle/2004-09-30-extended-a</u>dolescence_x.htm. Accessed. 1/13/13.

King, P. E. and R. W. Roeser. 2009. "Religion and Spirituality in Adolescent Development." In R. M. Lerner & L. Steinberg (Eds.) *Handbook of Adolescent Psychology*, (3rd edition). Wiley Publications. New York, NY.

Kupelian, David. 2005. *The Marketing of Evil.* WND Books, Cumberland House Publishing, Inc. Nashville, TN.

Leahy, Frederick S. 1990. *Satan Cast Out.* The Banner of Truth Trust. Carlisle, PA.

Liberty Alliance. 2012. "Fathers Disappear From Households Across America". Zionica.com. Accessed 12/31/12.

Littleton, Mark. 1988. *Submission is For Husbands, Too.* Accent Books. Denver, CO.

Malarek, Victor. 2003. "The Natashas." Arcade Publishing. New York, NY.

Mathewes-Green, Frederica. 1994. "Twice Liberated: A Personal Journey Through Feminism." *Touchstone Magazine,* Summer.

Meier, Paul D. 1998. *Christian Child-Rearing and Personality Development.* Baker Book House. Grand Rapids, MI.

Metaksa, Tanya. 1997. *Safe, Not Sorry.* Regan Books, a HarperCollins Imprint. New York, NY.

Murphy, Dr. Ed. 1992. *The Handbook for Spiritual Warfare.* Thomas Nelson Publishers. Nashville, TN.

National Institutes of Health. 2002. "Alcohol-related Traffic Deaths. http://www.nih.gov/about/researchresultsforthepublic/ AlcoholRelatedTrafficDeaths. PDF document. (Accessed August 22, 2009)

Ohlschlager, George and Ron Hawkins. 2001. "Toward A Clinical Theology of Marriage: Embracing Unifying Kingdom Values to Escape the Gender Wars in The Church." *Marriage and Family: A Christian Journal,* Vol. 4, Issue 1, 31–45.

Rosenbaum, Philip. 1994. *The Promise"* Broadman & Holman Publishers. Nashville, TN.

Sarason, Irwin G. and Barbara R. Sarason. 1999. *Abnormal Psychology.* Prentice Hall Publishers. Upper Saddle River, NJ.

Shaffer, Barbara W. 2005. "Emotional Abuse: Abuse beneath Abuse." *Christian Counseling Today.* Vol. 13, No. 3, pg. 20–23.

Slattery, Dr. Julianna. 2001. *Finding the Hero in Your Husband.* Health Communications. Deerfield Beach, FL.

Smalley, Gary and John Trent. 1993. *The Gift of the Blessing.* Thomas Nelson Publishers. Nashville, TN.

Survivors of Incest Anonymous. 2007. World Service Offices, Inc., www. siawso.org. Acessed November 2012.

Tauke, Beverly Hubble. 2004. *Overcoming the Sins of the Family.* Salt River—Tyndale House Publishers. Wheaton, IL.

Tenney, Merrill C., General Editor. 1978. "The Zondervan Pictorial Bible Dictionary." Zondervan Publishing House. Grand Rapids, MI.

United States Census Bureau. 2001. "Current Population Reports." Washington, D.C., 20–537, Table CH-5.

Vanier, Jean. 2003. *Community and Growth.* Paulist Press. New York, NY.

Wallerstein, Judith, Julia M. Lewis, and Sandra Blakeslee. 2000. *The Unexpected Legacy of Divorce: A 25 Year Landmark Study.* Hypcrion.

Warren, Rick. 2002. *The Purpose Driven Life.* Zondervan Publishing House. Grand Rapids, MI.

Zampino, Jean. 2004. "Radical Femininity—Part II." 2004. *Mastering Life Newsletter,* a ministry of Mastering Life Ministries, Jacksonville, FL. Num. 64, September.

About the Author

About the Author—Christian counselor Dr. Robert B. Shaw Jr. is a licensed professional counselor, dually licensed in Virginia and North Carolina, and a National Board Certified Counselor. He is also an ordained minister, serving as a youth pastor, Christian education director, adult education director, musician, and executive pastor in churches in New Jersey, Colorado, Maryland, and currently in North Carolina, for over twenty-five years. He has also been a middle school and high school teacher and athletic coach in both the public and private school environments. Dr. Shaw has spent several years counseling in church settings and community agencies and counseling military personnel and their families near Ft. Bragg, North Carolina. He specializes in trauma related issues; addictions; and victims of abuse, depression, anxiety disorders, life adjustment issues, loss, and grief, counseling church leaders and pastors, adolescents, and adults. Dr. Shaw's is a unique prophetic voice in the kingdom caring for hurting people, and he serves as an adjunct professor for a Christian university, an author, and a conference speaker. Dr. Shaw has a bachelor's degree in religious studies from Wagner College, New York and a master of divinity degree from Christian International Theological School, Florida. He also has a master of arts in professional counseling from Liberty University, Virginia and a doctor of ministry degree in formational counseling, a practical theology, from Ashland Theological Seminary, Ohio. He is a member of the American Association of Christian Counseling.

Dr. Shaw and his wife, Lorinda, have been married since 1978, and they have raised five children together. He loves running, sports, the beach, and spending time with family.

For contact information requests and speaking arrangements please send to – robertbshaw55@gmail.com